The Baby Face Killer & Other Stories of True Crime

Pete Bird

Published by DayBac Publishing, 2021.

While every precaution has been taken in the preparation of this book, the publisher assumes no responsibility for errors or omissions, or for damages resulting from the use of the information contained herein.

THE BABY FACE KILLER & OTHER STORIES OF TRUE CRIME

First edition. July 13, 2021.

Copyright © 2021 Pete Bird.

ISBN: 979-8224500987

Written by Pete Bird.

THE BABY FACE KILLER & OTHER STORIES OF TRUE CRIME

PETE BIRD

DAPHNE ABDELA

Some murders offer more questions than answers. The vicious slaying of Michael McMorrow, a forty-four-year-old real estate worker, is such a case. That his murder was carried out by fifteen-year-old kids is just one of the bizarre elements to the crime, which took place in the Strawberry Fields area of Central Park, New York City, in 1997.

Who actually wielded the blows that killed Michael? Was it Daphne Abdela, the rich girl gone bad? Or Christopher Vasquez, the boy from the other side of the tracks whose numerous emotional issues saw him placed on prescription drugs to help him cope with anxiety and depression? Or was it the two, egging each other on in a fit of alcohol fuelled frenzy?

What had happened in these young people's lives that they should turn to such crime at so young an age? Both, as far as could be told, came from loving families. Daphne in particular enjoyed every material benefit money could buy. But both still spent the latter half of their teen years behind bars.

Equally confusing was why a forty-four-year-old man had spent the late evening socialising with a couple of teens. Was it a meeting of pure innocence? Witnesses said that he often spent time with the youngsters and had been with them earlier that day. Is it just our cynical minds that steer us to wonder if there was some kind of ulterior motive in the casual drinking which took place?

In fact, will we ever know what actually occurred in the night-time nether world of the park? The murder of Michael McMorrow is a mysterious case. On the face of it, the facts are that a man died under a barrage of savage stab wounds and slices from a knife. As a consequence, two teenagers spent a few years in prison – a small sentence in comparison to the severity of their crime, but a large percentage of their young lives. We cannot help but feel that there is more to the killing of this middle-aged real estate worker than first meets the eye.

Daphne Abdela was adopted as a baby. Little is known about her biological parents (it is believe that they died while she was still extremely young); but she was adopted by a wealthy couple, Angelo Abdela, a senior executive with a large food company, and his wife Catherine, who had been a model and was French born. They lived in a sumptuous apartment overlooking Central Park.

It seems a reasonable assumption to make that had she stayed with her biological parents Daphne may have grown up in a state of impoverishment. Instead, she became the spoiled little rich girl, provided with every toy and treat for which she could wish. But something was wrong. Daphne was not a loving girl thankful for her comfortable life. Nor was she even one who simply accepted her good fortune. Daphne was disturbed. Extremely so.

There was an example when she was just eight or nine years old. Clearly, it was not the first sign that all was not well with the young girl, and certainly not the last, but it does perhaps illustrate the problems that were to come.

Gail Slatter was a swimming mom. She would take her daughter to the pool at the YMCA on West 63rd Street, and one of that daughter's teammates was Daphne Abdela. Nine-year olds can be terribly precocious; they can be nauseatingly self-centred and cause their parents to dream of the day they begin to grow up. However, they are also still little kids, they tend to do as they are told (eventually) and they tend to love their parents deep down, even if sometimes that is hard to deduce.

Daphne Abdela was different. 'She wasn't a happy, jolly, jumping around type of person like the other kids,' recalls Gail. She was not able to make friends with her swimming mates on the team. In fact, it was as though she had no wish to do so. 'The consensus of the kids was that she was strange,' continued the former swimming mom.

But it was her relationship towards her mother that seemed most odd. Ms Slatter recalls how the little girl would walk a short distance in front of Catherine, rather as though she was some kind of dignitary, and her mother was a necessary but unwanted bodyguard – someone to be tolerated as a necessary evil but neither respected nor especially liked.

'Daphne would walk three feet in front of her mother,' recalls Gail. 'She seemed like a bully to her mother. Daphne never smiled; she never laughed. After she got out of the pool, the child would come over and the mother couldn't get close to her. Her mother would ask her things and Daphne was always unresponsive. She would ignore her.'

It seemed to the other moms that Catherine Abdela was frightened of her daughter. Perhaps embarrassed by her as well. 'She seemed intimated by her,' Gail remembers. On top of this, Daphne was extremely strong willed. The swimming coach at the YMCA was strict, and the golden rule was that, however much criticism, advice or yelling took place, the kids kept swimming. They all did. Except for the rich young girl with the adoptive parents.

If Daphne was annoyed, or tired, or just felt like stopping she would. There and then in the water her feet would go down, or if her diminutive frame could not reach the bottom, she would grab the side. It was not that she was struggling with her swimming, she was a talented girl in that respect, but simply she wished to stop, for whatever reason, so she did.

The swimming team had a good reputation in the community. It was a diverse gathering that went under the name of the West Side Marlins. Heather Morelli was a team-mate of Daphne. She spent four years in the side with her, but like all of the other boys and girls who swam together, felt that she could not break through the thick veneer that shielded Daphne from others of her age.

'She was very hard and difficult. I don't know how to say it,' said Heather, who swam with Daphne in the early nineties. 'She was very independent. She didn't mold to anything. She didn't have her own groove.

An incident occurred which stuck in the mind of many parents who recalled the time Daphne spent on the swimming team. One day Daphne became upset and launched a racist attack on a black child who was a part of the group. It is not acceptable, but kids do this kind of thing. Usually, afterwards they are sorry for their outburst.

There was no indication that such behaviour was tolerated within the family. Indeed, both parents had foreign backgrounds. On top of Catherine's French heritage, Angelo was an Israeli. As was so often the case, Catherine was dismayed and embarrassed by her daughter's outburst. She remonstrated firmly and tried to get her daughter to apologise. She would not do so. Ever.

'I got the impression that the parents found her a touch kid to control,' said another parent from the time, who wished to remain anonymous. 'She did what she wanted.'

In many ways, it was not even as though the young Daphne disliked her mother. More, it was as though she regarded the carer as socially below her. Daphne's world seemed hierarchical, with her at the top and only servants existing below her. Generally, to dislike somebody, there must be a relationship of sorts with them. Some kind of bond which has gone sour. It seemed as though Daphne had never established that bond with her parents.

Even in the most terrible of homes, where abuse – physical and sexual – combine with neglect to leave children permanently damaged, the relationship from a young child towards their parents is different. There remains a trust and a love. This is why often domestic abuse involving children goes undetected for so long; kids feel a loyalty towards their parents, and a need to protect them.

There is absolutely no suggestion that any kind of abusive situation of any sort occurred within the Abdela home. Every indicator showed that Angelo and Catherine adored their child, caring for her to the absolute best of their ability.

Certainly, Angelo worked long hours; he had a high-profile job and like many in his position managing work and home life was an almost impossible mix. He rarely if ever attended swimming meets, for example, but Catherine was always there. Many families find keeping up with the struggles of daily life puts a strain on the time they can spend with their children. In the Abdela's case, things were better than for most. At least Angelo brought in the kind of salary that enabled them to live a millionaire's lifestyle with Catherine able to devote every moment to her daughter.

But the kind of antipathy a child feels towards a parent, such as was demonstrated in the examples at the swimming pool listed above, do not happen overnight. They are symptomatic of a long period of problems.

And it seems that family relationships did not improve.

Five or six years later Daphne was sitting in her Upper West Side apartment eating a bowl of mac and cheese. There was a knock on the door – the police had arrived to interview her. Angelo pleaded with her to say nothing until she had a lawyer present. But Daphne treated him with the same disdain she had shown towards her mother all those years ago, in fact with the same disregard and disrespect she always displayed towards both of them. She insisted that he should not be present while the police spoke to her. But she was a minor, and on this occasion her tantrum drew no response.

The girl had advanced beyond stamping her feet at the poolside. By now, it seemed, her parents were genuinely afraid of her. Her behaviour had escalated downwards to such an extent that her father had recently been forced to take a restraining order out against her.

She was verbally and physically abusive to both her mom and dad. She had attended and left a series of expensive and prestigious schools.

In fact, her parents had just removed her from the latest costly institution, the Loyola School.

As she got older, she had taken to skipping out at night to enter the nearby Central Park, where she would drink with the aging hippies, homeless 'Parkers' and others who inhabit the nether world of the refreshing green oxygen tank after dark. This is a side sheltered from the thousands who jog along the park's lanes or enjoy its beauty as an oasis in a busy city by day. Indeed, it was because her parents could not get her out of the park that they had sought the restraining order, and had a curfew imposed upon her.

One regular user of the park was Michael McMorrow. He lived with his elderly mother and had a problem with alcohol. Indeed, he and Daphne had met at a therapy session some months before. Now the two often shared a drink in the darkness with other of the park's night-time inhabitants. A forty-four-year-old man with a fifteen-year-old girl? Our minds inevitably turn to dark thoughts, but there is little, perhaps none at all, evidence that the relationship was anything other than a slightly weird acquaintanceship.

Some reports state that McMorrow attempted a drunken kiss on Daphne the night he died; but if that is the case, it seems that Daphne carried no ill will about it. Indeed, the claim could simply be another example of the uncertain information surrounding this crime.

It was in Central Park that Daphne met the other significant person in this story – Christopher Vasquez. It seems as though Daphne, dressed in the 'grunge' clothes emblazoned with designer labels so popular with wealthy kids who would like to appear otherwise, was taken with Christopher. He was the same age as she, but from a much less affluent home. He lived with his mother in a run-down apartment block on the other side of the park. Although he was a former altar boy who attended the well-regarded Beekman School, Christopher wanted to be a rebel. Sometimes, he would carry a knife, which he would produce secretively, as though confused by a combination of wanting to show it off, and fear that he might be caught carrying it.

Christopher's was a sad case. His parents were split, and he suffered from both anxiety and depression. He had been on medication for many years. He was a small, slender kid, with the spotty face of an adolescent. Initially it is hard to see quite the attraction between Daphne and him. But then again, perhaps their relationship is easier to explain when it is thought about.

Both loved roller blading and would skate through the park together. Christopher was soon besotted by his female friend, and she in turn loved the opportunity to have a boy at her beck and call. There is no doubt that he was full of adolescent lust for her; the extent to which those feelings were reciprocated is harder to ascertain; it seems as though she would entice him one moment and reject him the next. Given that he was just fifteen years old, descriptions of the young boy are often far from kindly. He was a child who seemed to naturally attract the attentions of bullies – child and adult.

He appeared in Stella Sand's account of the crime, along with Daphne, under a sensationalist title 'Baby Faced Butchers'; to be fair to Sand, the moniker was borrowed from the name given to the pair by the gutter press. Adolescence treated him harshly. One friend, speaking at the time and who wished to remain nameless, said that Vasquez tried to join a gang. When he succeeded, his personality changed.

'He was never in school. He punched my friend in the face at his party for no reason.' This was a boy struggling with the changes wrought by his age. He suffered from the greasiness of puberty; his hair was often lank, and he wore unfashionable clothes, perhaps because (unlike his occasional girlfriend), he could afford no better. He would drink, take drugs and smoke with Daphne. She had a big problem with alcohol; she even attended Alcoholics Anonymous, although she was just fifteen at the time. She was assigned a counsellor to help her through the difficulties, but such support only works if the patient is prepared to go along with the treatment, something Abdela was too immature, too self-centred and too mixed up to contemplate at that stage. It seems, though, from what happened on that May evening, that Daphne could hold her liquor better than her part time boyfriend.

For a girl like Daphne who needed to feel in charge, he was the perfect friend – one she could manipulate and dominate.

And so, on May 22nd, 1997, matters reached their head. Daphne was in a particularly tense mood. She told friends, if that is the right word for the people with whom she mixed, that she 'was going to kill someone tonight.' Although, this was a boast she often made. Allegedly, she was carrying a switchblade, and told her boyfriend that she was going to 'slice someone.'

Drinking and smoking, the two come across Michael Morrow with a group of 'Parkers' telling a story. He is drinking himself. They persuade him to go with them. They end up at the lake located in this part of the park. Abdela has a pack of beers with her, and she gives one to the older man. The question has to be asked once more, why was he drinking with a couple of kids late at night? Friends describe Michael as kindly; they call him a helpful person, always on the look out to lend a hand when it is needed. He is funny and does a fine comic impression of the actor Kirk Douglas. He works hard and looks after his elderly mother.

But still, he is drinking with two fifteen-year olds in the late hours in a darkened park. Some teens, girls in particular, can easily pass for much older women, but not Daphne, nor for that matter, Christopher. In lots of ways, he is still a little boy, clearly a minor. She too is one who looks younger than her years. As is the fashion of the time, she dresses her age as well.

Down at the lake, something happens. Two witnesses who were in the group with whom Michael was sharing his story report that he and Daphne went off somewhere by themselves, and Christopher became distressed, angry and animated, demanding 'Where are they?' both loudly and repeatedly. But how reliable this testimony might be is open to question.

In any case, some trigger happens, and Michael is stabbed repeated and violently. He is slashed across the throat, and cuts to his face are so severe that his nose is almost severed. He is stabbed in his most intimate parts. This is a crime that is motivated by something more than just alcohol. The killer is disturbed. There can be no doubt. That he, or she, or they are just fifteen years old is even more distressing. Then, as Michael lay dying, his stomach is hacked open with the knife, and filled with stones from nearby. He is pushed into the lake, the stones intended to weigh him down. When his body is discovered the next day, there are several feet of intestines floating nearby.

Daphne Abdela later claimed that Christopher had lost his temper, and committed the crime, while she had attempted to stop him, and had even attempted resuscitation on the dying man. Vasquez, for his part, argued that he had been egged on by the girl he admired so much. She had helped send the victim sprawling to the ground the easier to cut away at his body. She had told Vasquez to 'slice him (McMorrow) from ear to ear.'

With their victim dying, they rush back to Abdela's apartment block, where they try to wash away the blood from their bodies in the basement maintenance room. Meanwhile, Angelo Abdela is worried about his daughter's whereabouts. Once more she has broken the conditions of her curfew and he calls the police to report her missing.

The police arrive to find the couple cleaning themselves off; they claim to have fallen badly while roller blading and, with most of McMorrow's blood now off their bodies, the police believe their story.

However, later that night, an emergency call is made claiming that there is a body in the lake. It is easily traced to Abdela's home, and she is arrested. Soon, Vasquez is also assisting police with their enquiries.

When the matter came to court, Daphne's father hired the best defence money could buy. Benjamin Brafman was a young lawyer gaining a reputation. He would go on to defend Harvey Weinstein before quitting in the face of his client's attitude. He was also Michael Jackson's attorney.

Together with the DA's office, it is decided not to press for murder charges, and Daphne ends up with a ten-year sentence for manslaughter. The same sentence was given to Christopher Vasquez, and each served six years of their punishment, before being released in 2004.

Daphne returned to live with her father – her mother died just prior to her release from prison. Shortly after her release, a note was found on a bench donated as a memorial to Michael McMorrow. Signed 'D', it apologised to the victim for his death, and once more claimed that an attempt had been made to save his life. Handwriting experts confirmed that the note was from Daphne.

It seems, indeed, that Daphne might have had some redeeming features in her personality. At one point in her school career, she attended the Columbia Grammar and Preparatory School. 'She was a good kid from a good family,' Richard J Soghoian, the school's headmaster, told the New York Times. 'As far as I am concerned, I am very surprised,' he said after Daphne's trial. 'She has wonderful parents.'

However, some of Mr Soghoian's glowing account is a little compromised by the fact that he could not recall the actual years she had attended his school. Perhaps he knew the girl a little less well than he was letting on.

The final years of the last millennium marked a strange time in the criminal history of the USA. It was a period when murders by children – teenagers - started to become almost commonplace. On top of the vicious crime carried out by Daphne and Christopher, other appalling acts hit the headlines.

Among the more notorious, in 1997 Melissa Draxler, a promising student with a deeply caring family murdered her baby, a child she had kept secret from her parents, friends and even the child's father. After killing the new-born – she gave birth in a toilet – she returned to the dance floor of a prom she was attending. Jeremy Strohmeyer was a teen who raped and murdered a seven-year-old girl. Afterwards, he left and continued his lavish lifestyle.

He too came from a privileged background. A rich kid gone wrong. We could go on for a long time with similar stories; Amy Grossberg and Brian Peterson, two kids from comfortable backgrounds who murdered their son; Corey Arthur, like Christopher Vasquez, a boy from a challenging part of New York, who killed his teacher.

These are not gang killings; they are not necessarily drug or alcohol fuelled, although a dependence on these is sometimes a consequence of the anti-social behaviour the kids display. Nor is the easy excuse of disinterested parents or abusive relationships relevant in this explosion of unpleasantness. Psychologist Dr David Hartman has a theory, and it is one that sits uncomfortably with some parents. Hartman was director of neuropsychology at the Isaac Ray Centre for Psychiatry and Law in Chicago. He is a man whose views are worthy of time and consideration.

'The young people involved in some of these violent acts are without the capacity to make the connection with another life,' he suggests. 'They need have no more reason for hurting another person than they have for peeling an orange.'

Another psychologist, Michael Schulman (who wrote the book 'Bringing Up a Moral Child) offers a similar explanation for this kind of crime. 'You need to teach the child that the family stands for goodness and not simply for comfort and intellectual achievement, but that moral excellence is honoured,'

Clearly, the implication from Schulman and Hartman is that despite the material advantages from which Daphne Abdela (and others who go on to commit serious crimes) benefitted, there was a lack of moral substance in their household. The values with which she was imbued were insufficient to lead her to be able to empathise with others.

Perhaps that is the case; the examples of young killers listed above were made up of many kids from comfortable backgrounds. But is it also not the case that it is easy to blame rich parents? Is there not a kind of social morality whereby those of us from 'ordinary' backgrounds hold a little envy towards those blessed with a greater variety of creature comforts?

Thus, we rather like the idea that for all their wealth, parents such as these are not very good at the job of parenting. They may be experts in their professional fields, but the most important job of all, the one that society depends on most – the job of bringing up kids to become valuable members of society – is one that we are better at than they?

There are certainly many who would buy into the idea that the likes of Schulman and Hartman are simply tapping into a ready audience of people who are happy enough to blame the upper echelons of our society for its ills.

There are other reasons that may go some way to explaining why both Daphne Abdela and Christopher Vasquez, or maybe just one of them, killed a man on that evening in the dark of Central Park.

And those reasons lie around the field of mental illness. In many ways, it is easier to use this explanation for Christopher Vasquez. We have hard evidence of his poor emotional state, and clear information about the pills he took to address this. Studies now show that anti-depressants can have serious side effects, and these are magnified when the user is a child. Studies have demonstrated an increased risk of suicide in children prescribed the drugs.

Even more alarming is a study printed in a PLOS Medicine, a respected medical journal, which found that teenagers were more than fifty per cent more likely to commit serious crime: robbery, rape, assault - and homicide - if on anti-depressants. That study is not alone in its findings.

But back in the late 1990s such knowledge was rare in doctors. Could it be that Christopher Vasquez was an alienated child, one on the fringes of his peer groups, but only committed a frenzied killing because of the influence of the drugs he was instructed to take?

At the same time, Daphne Abdela did not experience a normal childhood; something that does not seem to have been her parents' fault, but it is undoubtedly the case that mental illness in the 1990s was a little understood condition. Might there have been something within her own make up that led her to become the anti-social child she undoubtedly was?

We can only suppose. Maybe she and Christopher were just bad people, teens without the empathy to truly understand what it means to take a life. More likely they were, in their own ways, victims themselves. Sufferers whom society was unprepared, and unable, to treat.

KILLER TEEN NIKKI REYNOLDS

15

SAMANTHA REED

It is not often that stories appear where we find the perpetrators of violence being children and the victims being parents. Although, scattered throughout history it has been seen that children can be capable of shocking amounts of violence, and many, assuming their innocent nature, fall victim to them. In Coral Springs, Florida in 1997 one such story took place. And still the actions of the evening resonate throughout the community.

In The Beginning

Born in 1979 to a mother that didn't want her, Jacquiline "Nikki" Reynolds was adopted by Robert and Billie Jean Reynolds three months after her birth. The Reynolds were a loving, Christian family from Coral Springs, Florida and they were delighted to welcome their new daughter into their lives.

There was nothing that they wouldn't do for Nikki. Robert Reynolds worked for the Department of Transportation and Billie Jean was an administrative assistant at RJ Reynolds. They had a quiet home and they were devoted to making their daughter happy.

Nikki was a good child. She was devoted to the church, like her parents, and she loved her parents deeply. She would go to the mall with her mother or watch baseball games with her father. She could never spend too much time with them. The Reynolds did everything to ensure that Nikki was being raised in a loving and non-judgmental environment.

Friends and family would agree that the environment was loving, but the Reynolds gave Nikki everything she wanted. She was pampered, she was spoiled, and in the end, she was a bit of a brat. Sometimes the best intentions can have the worst consequences.

Still, Nikki, as she got older, became a good student and didn't act out. She achieved good grades in school and went out of her way to become involved in extra curricular activities. She also stayed heavily involved with the church alongside her parents.

By all appearances, Nikki was the perfect child. She was the child that most parents dream of having and Robert and Billie Jean were delighted with her. But children grow up, despite anything that their parents try to do to stop it, and Nikki was no exception. And not all children grow up in a manner that their parents can be proud of.

The Beginning of the End

Nikki went from being the model child to what most people would call a 'troubled teen'. It didn't start in the way one would expect, with failing grades and a lack of interest in school. It started with a lie, and one that shocked family and friends in the disturbing nature of it.

In 1996, sixteen-year-old Nikki came home from school and claimed that she had been assaulted after getting off of the school bus. Naturally her parents were shocked and appalled to hear that this had happened to her. They immediately called the police to handle the situation officially. Nikki claimed she had been attacked by someone she knew, at first. But when questioned by the police her story quickly changed.

She went on to say that she didn't know her attacker and then that the attack hadn't happened at all. She hadn't been raped. She'd made the whole story up.

Now why would a sixteen-year-old, devote Christian girl make up a story about being raped? Why would she go to the extreme of telling her parents and getting the police involved if it was just a story?

It turns out that Nikki hadn't been raped. Rather she was in a relationship, the first one of a sexual nature in her lifetime, and she was terrified to tell her parents about it. She was worried about what they would think about their daughter sacrificing her morals and her principles just to have a boyfriend. But Carlos Infante was her entire world. The sixteen-year-old classmate was consuming her life focus to the point that she hadn't hesitated to throw caution to the wind.

And when the thought of telling her parents about what was going on had come up, in her mind, fabricating a rape story had seemed like a better idea. Nikki was also concerned that she might be pregnant, a worry that was quickly put to rest, but it also influenced her decision to pursue the rape narrative.

Billie Jean was extremely unhappy with Nikki, potentially for the first time during her parenting of the girl. She didn't like the fact that Nikki had a boyfriend. She didn't like the fact that she'd sacrificed her principles and morals, the beliefs that they thought they'd instilled into her all for some boy. They believed that they'd raised a good, Christian girl and for the first time they were starting to question that belief.

Bille Jean and Robert disliked the idea of Nikki having a boyfriend, it didn't particularly matter who he was. They viewed it as a step down for her. They saw it as a complete abandonment of her belief system, something they had strived to instill in her over the course of her entire life. She was sacrificing everything in order to be with this boy, from their point of view. She was losing herself in him. And Billie Jean and Robert wanted to help get Nikki back on a clear path, on a Christian path.

So, they insisted that she spend less time with Carlos and more time with the church. They hoped that in doing so she would see her wrongdoings and find her true self again. They hoped that in spending more time with the church that she would become closer to the family again and forget about Carlos.

Billie Jean believed that Nikki needed to spend more time with a better group of people, a Christian group of people. She hoped that if Nikki spent time around other good, Christian kids that she would find her way again, that she would find a better crowd. And Billie Jean was willing to go to great lengths to ensure that her daughter found a path that fit with the beliefs and morals of the family.

But sometimes the child, no matter how much they push, cannot realize the hopes and dreams of parents. And sometimes, despite all efforts, things still go wrong.

Rebellion Continues

Teenage rebellion can be a strong force, however, and the more that Billie Jean pushed Nikki to go to church the more she resisted. Nikki said, "I knew that the way I was living was not right in God's eyes, but I did not want to hear all of that." She was too engulfed in her life with Carlos. He was quickly becoming her entire world and nothing else mattered to her. Not her parents, and certainly not her church.

The rebellion was extending into her school life. Nikki, who had once been a good student with marks that her parents could be proud of was now beginning to skip class. Her grades were beginning to fall as a result and she was no longer the academic force that she was before.

It was to the point that Billie Jean and Robert barely recognized the girl that they had raised anymore. Who was this young woman living in their house? She reflected none of the morals and principles they had raised her to uphold. She wouldn't listen to them. She opposed them at every turn. They began to wonder what had happened to their daughter Nikki. Where had she gone?

Nikki went from a happy-go-lucky child that was a pleasure to be around, a child who was soft spoken and loved to go to church to a girl no one could recognize. She wore dark clothes, she changed her music, she changed her bedroom to dark colours – she became the opposite of herself. It was hard to tell if this was simply teenage rebellion or something more going on. Was this all because of Carlos or was there some deeper problem at play?

She slept a lot, more than any teenager should and she isolated herself from her family. Gone were the days of ice cream and base ball games. She no longer went on trips to the mall with her mother. She no longer went to church with her family. She became disinterested in many things that used to hold her attention, things that used to captivate her. Her whole world now revolved around Carlos.

It was her first sexual relationship with anyone in her life and it had reached the point of obsession. She filled her diary with everything to do with Carlos. Her room was plastered with photos of him. Her every waking moment revolved around him. There was an unnatural intensity to her emotions towards him, an unhealthy intensity. And it was quickly becoming evident that this was a problem.

Naturally, Billie Jean and Robert were very concerned about their daughter's current mental state. She was not herself, and the only thing they could blame was Carlos as he was the only changing factor in her life. It seemed that he was a negative influence on Nikki in many ways. He didn't make good grades as a student, and now her grades were plummeting as well.

Billie Jean was also worried that he was coming over every day, potentially when they were at work. They had no way to confirm this, but she didn't like the idea that he was at the house alone with her while they were at work. It didn't sit well with her.

So Billie Jean put her foot down, perhaps for the first time in her experience as a parent. She began to tell Nikki no, especially when it came to Carlos. And Nikki handled it with the maturity level of a toddler as opposed to that of a teenager. Nikki threw awful tantrums. Billie Jean and Nikki would engage in screaming matches in the house that would result in slammed doors. The result was very wearing on Billie Jean. She found herself screaming at Nikki almost all of the time. This was not what she wanted her life as a mother to be. This was not the girl she had raised. She needed to do something about this, but she was at a loss as to what the solution could be.

And despite the screaming matches and the orders to stay away, Nikki still kept seeing Carlos. It seemed that nothing could keep her from Carlos. She would sneak out at night when everyone was asleep to see him and it didn't matter what the consequences were.

Billie Jean's frustration escalated to the point that one day she confided in a friend saying "Don't be surprised if one day you come home and there's police cars and fire trucks up and down the street 'cause one of us, it'll be me or Nikki, but one of us will be gone."

Billie Jean's prediction would prove to hit a little too close to home in the coming days. And the aftermath would shock everyone.

Intervention

It was May 14, 1997 when the school counselor contacted Billie Jean to tell her that there was trouble with Nikki and Carlos. She asked that Billie Jean come in and speak with her in person and that Billie Jean, Robert, and Nikki come in for a full meeting the next day. Upon visiting the high school, the counselor told Billie Jean that Nikki and Carlos had more than just the usual high school relationship issues to deal with.

That day Nikki had told the counselor that she was pregnant with Carlos' baby. This had naturally prompted the counselor to contact Billie Jean immediately about the issue. Billie Jean, having already dealt with Nikki's questionable honesty with the previous rape accusation, was hesitant to believe the pregnancy claim. She was fairly certain that this was another one of Nikki's schemes, but there was a sure way to determine its legitimacy.

So she took Nikki to the drug store to find out what was what.

The results of the pregnancy test were negative. That didn't mean Billie Jean was any less pleased with her daughter. Nikki called Carlos with the news. And despite having a counseling meeting the next day Billie Jean decided to seek guidance from a higher power. She dragged Nikki away from the phone and took Nikki to see the church counselor.

Nikki spoke with her pastor as they waited to see the counselor. He was supportive as he talked to her about her boyfriend problems and offered her guidance. Their conversation with the counselor did not have the same supportive tone. The counselor spent the session telling Nikki that her mother did not deserve the behaviour she was displaying. She raised her voice and yelled at Nikki. This didn't go over very well.

Nikki removed herself from the office and from the church. She wanted nothing more to do with the impromptu counseling session. And as she stood in the parking lot of the church she even debated removing herself from the family by running away. But she didn't run away, however. Instead, she took a higher ground, something that hadn't been seen from her in almost a year. She went back into the counselor's office and apologized to her mother. And she finished the session with the counselor before returning home with her mother.

Billie Jean believed that they had made a step in the right direction. She would be the one to learn how wrong she was about that fact.

Confusion and Confessions

It was barely an hour after their visit to the counselor on May 14, 1997 that the call came in to 911. At 7:07pm Nikki Reynolds' panicked voice came over the phone saying "I stabbed her repeatedly in the back. There's blood all over her and all over the floor and everything."

Police were at her house in minutes and the scene that they witnessed was one that would stay with some of the officers for years after. When police arrived they found Nikki waiting on her doorstep. One of the officers who responded indicated that "She had blood all over, blood on her legs, blood on her face."

Nikki was placed in the back of the police car and left to wait while the police went to investigate. A tape recorder was left on with her in the police car so that anything that was said while she was alone was recorded and on file. It recorded her praying that her mother was still be alive and saying that she had learned her lesson. She was asking God to forgive her and for her mother to please still be alive.

Her mother was brought out of the house on a stretcher by the EMTs and she was still alive at the time that she left the house. However, Billie Jean was pronounced dead at the hospital at 8:10pm after suffering from 13 stab wounds.

Nikki was taken to the police department immediately. Robert came home from work to find the house in a state of chaos, surrounded by police cars and police tape. He hadn't yet been informed of the situation that had come to pass behind the front doors of his home. He broke down at the news that his wife was gone and that his daughter was responsible. The shock of it was something that he couldn't quite comprehend.

The scene inside the house was gruesome and shocking to police investigators. It depicted Billie Jean's terrible, drawn out death as she fought to get away from her daughter. But there was no escape for her as she was stabbed repeatedly until she finally lay immobile on the floor.

The police found the kitchen knife that had been used as the murder weapon in the sink and it still had blood on it. They also found evidence that someone, likely Nikki, had attempted to clean up the scene using towels and dishcloths. The blood soaked pieces of cloth were scattered about the kitchen unable to handle the sheer amount of blood that had resulted from the incident.

While the police officers worked diligently at the crime seen the detectives questioned Nikki about the murder. And it didn't take too much effort to get her to talk.

"I didn't have any intentions of lying." Nikki said. "I didn't have any secrets. I wanted to get it out." She felt almost compelled to tell the story of what had happened. She needed to let them know.

"It was simple, all I had to ask her was what happened today and just started chatting. She went through the whole story from a to b," said the detective who interviewed Nikki.

The story that was told by Nikki revolved heavily around Carlos Infante, the infamous boyfriend. Nikki had used her fake pregnancy to keep Carlos in a relationship with her when he wanted to leave, fearing what would happen if he left. When she had found out she was not pregnant, for sure, she called him to give the news. Carlos indicated that he wanted nothing to do with her and all of her lies. He'd had enough. Billie Jean had even got on the phone with Carlos and apologized for all of the drama that he'd had to endure at the hands of her daughter.

Nikki had decided then and there that someone would die that day. She even took a handful of aspirin before going to the counseling meeting with her mother at the church. She was certain that she could overdose on it. She was certain that it would be her that would die.

However, when the overdose failed her thoughts went from suicide to homicide rather quickly. But the intended victim had not been her mother.

Her plan had been to get a hold of Carlos the next day and kill him. She figured she could catch him after first hour and slash his throat if she snuck up behind him. She believed that if she couldn't have him then no one should be allowed to have him. He belonged to her essentially.

However, the one obstacle in her plan to kill Carlos was the meeting they had with the guidance counselor the next day. Nikki was unsure whether she would be sent home after the meeting or not. In order to kill Carlos she would have to skip the guidance meeting. So, in order to accomplish this, she figured she would have to kill her parents as well. She would just wait until they were sleeping and then simply slash their throats. Then they could no longer stand in her way.

A real obstacle came into this metaphorical plan when her father left for church after dinner that night alone and her mother stayed home. This was very out of character for them. Nikki also stayed home as her mother told her she was grounded for the rest of the evening. She was instructed to clean the dishes after dinner.

Nikki decided that she would just roll with this change. She believed, since she was now home alone with her mother, that it would be much easier to kill her mother now, clean up the mess, and then wait until her father returned. She could then kill him and do the same. Finally, she could drive herself to school in the morning, wait for Carlos, and kill him after first hour just like she had planned. It would work out perfectly.

Logical thought was gone at this point in time. Nikki was acting strictly on whatever thoughts came to her mind and they were frantic, desperate. Still, she waited for her opportunity to arrive. She waited for her moment when she could kill her mother.

Opportunity came while she was cleaning up in the kitchen and Billie Jean was working at her computer. Nikki took a kitchen knife, paused for a moment to check the blade for its sharpness, and then slowly approached her mother. She hesitated now that she had the knife in hand. She wasn't sure what it would feel like to slash someone's throat.

When she finally got up the nerve to come up behind her mother and attempt to cut her throat it didn't slash it, it only cut it. Billie Jean jumped up in surprise and darted towards the laundry room. She screamed, "No, Nikki, no."

"I told her I had to kill her because I can't live without Carlos," Nikki explained to police in her interview.

Nikki kept stabbing her because she wanted to put her out of her misery, she claims. She didn't want her mother to suffering any longer. And in her last moments, Billie Jean still offered her daughter forgiveness for killing her.

Nikki spent one night in the hospital because of her claim of ingesting a large amount of Aspirin. After that she was turned over to the county jail where she was formally booked on a charge of First Degree Murder.

The First Trial

The first trial for Nikki Reynolds lasted from April 14, 1999 – May 3, 1999.

If convicted, Nikki faced life in prison after spending two years in a Juvenile Detention Centre. The prosecution built their case around Nikki's obsession with Carlos Infante, making sure to indicate that he was not at fault in any way and rather he was also one of the three listed on Nikki's kill list.

The defence opted to take an insanity plea route, rather than try to dispute the charge that Nikki had committed the murder – something she had confessed to multiple times. This defence fell flat. The criterion for an insanity plea is very strict. The accused has to suffer from a serious mental illness and the accused has to be unaware that what they are doing is wrong or has consequences.

The psychologist that testified for the prosecution indicated that Nikki was well aware of what she was doing, and rather that she was just a confused girl. The defence tried to argue that Nikki suffered from Borderline Personality disorder. They claimed that individuals suffering from this disorder could idolize the individuals they are with and then suddenly snap, and become violent. Which is very similar to Nikki's reaction after Carlos indicated he wanted nothing to do with her. They also claimed that the Aspirin played a part as Aspirin can cause metabolic imbalances and psychosis upon overdoes.

Regardless of the claims on either side, the jury was hung and the trial ended in a mistrial.

The Second Trial

Second trail for Nikki Reynolds began on Sept 1, 1999.

Similar to the first, the prosecution brought a series of psychologists to the stand to prove that, while not a rational act, Nikki was not insane. The prosecution also claimed that her mother's death was premeditated.

The defence countered that Nikki was mentally ill and called experts to speak to Nikki's sanity. The defence also brought forward Nikki's biological mother to testify. The birth mother had a long history of mental illness and family violence. The defence argued that it was the anxiety over losing Carlos that pushed Nikki over the edge and brought her mental illness to the surface.

After much deliberation, Nikki Reynolds was found guilty of Second Degree Murder at the end of the trial.

At the sentencing hearing on January 7, 2000 Nikki's biological mother made a plea to include treatment as a part of Nikki's sentence. She believed that her daughter needed help, much like she had needed help in her lifetime.

Nikki also addressed the court, pleading with the judge to sentence her to a psychiatric facility instead of prison. She truly believed that there had been something wrong that day, if not insanity, than something else. She believed that she needed help. She bore no ill will towards her family. She hated none of them. She had never hated them and still didn't.

However, the judge believed that the wrongness of what she had done to outweigh all else. He gave her the maximum sentence under Florida law, 34 years in prison. She was resentenced to 21 years and 8 months on April 4, 2001 due to a change in sentencing laws in the state of Florida.

In the end Robert Reynolds remarried in 1998 and has had no contact with his daughter since she was sent to prison on January 2000.

And Nikki was incarcerated at the Gadsden Correctional Facility in Quincy, Florida. She was eligible for parole in 2015 and was released.

BABY KILLER

The True Story of Amelia Dyer

Chrissy Eubank

Amelia Dyer, considered one of the most prolific serial killers in history, was born around 1837 in Victorian Britain. Her picture on the front cover easily betrays the evil that resided within her heart. Her reign of terror lasted over twenty years, as she is projected to have killed as many as 400 children before finally being caught

She embarked on a thirty year career of killing with eyewitnesses seeing at least six babies entering her house a day. The count of 400 dead is a conservative estimate.

EARLY LIFE

Amelia was the youngest of five children born into the tiny town of Pyle Marsh. She had three older brothers, Thomas, James, and William along with an older sister named Ann. Her father was a shoemaker named Samuel Hobley and her mother was named Sarah Weymouth.

But he didn't come from an impoverished family like so many others during the Victorian Era.

"For the time, she had a pretty good start," said author Allison Rattle. "Her father had a pretty good trade and paid for her to go to church and school which at the time only a quarter of the children her age actually got an education so she was privileged in that respect."

She found entertainment in reading and used to write poetry herself. Amelia's mother Sarah, however, became mentally ill after suffering from typhus fever. Amelia had to suffer through watching her mother's seizures and outbursts, providing care for her until she died in 1848.

"She witnessed her mother basically losing her mind," said Rattle. "And dying a slow, horrific death. I guess being a young girl she may have been called upon to nurse her mother slightly or at least wait upon her."

Psychologists have posited that it was going through this trauma of watching her mother lose her mind, that caused Amelia's own emotional wiring to run askew.

"Amelia would later claim that her mother died as a result of hereditary insanity," said author Allison Vale. "I think though that this isn't true but it's really easy to understand how she could have remembered it that way."

"It was certain to have a massive impact on her and she may have learned a few things about what kind of symptoms might be shown by someone whose losing their mind."

Amelia was sent to live with her aunt in nearby Bristol after her mother's death. She started an apprenticeship with a corset maker and worked there until her father died in 1859. The oldest brother, Thomas, took control of the family shoe business. Two years later, some type of estrangement occurred with her brothers, specifically James and Amelia doesn't appear to have further ties with her family.

In 1861, Amelia moved to Trinity Street, Bristol. She married George Thomas, who at 59 years old was 35 years Amelia's senior. The two lied about their ages on their marriage certificate with George claiming he was 48 years old and Amelia claiming she was 30.

A CAREER IN "HEALTH CARE"

Amelia began training as a nurse after she got married.

"Amelia turned to one of the most arduous professions she could have turned to," Vale said. "Nursing was just starting to change. It was post-Crimean war. Nursing was starting to have a much better profile as a result of Florence Nightingale. But it was still a thankless profession."

"It wasn't a caring profession like it is present day," agreed psychologist Laura Richards. "They train you psychologically to be a lot more robust around dealing with people. So she became quite hardy and emotionless from having been trained through the nursing regime."

Amelia became pregnant at the age of twenty-six before she met a woman named Ellen Dane who came to boarder at her house. Dane was a midwife who told her of a lucrative and shady way to earn money. Amelia would use her own home as a front to provide housing for women who had gotten pregnant out of wedlock. They would them give the babies away for adoption or kill them through malnutrition.

They called it baby farming.

"Amelia could see it was a very easy way to make money," Rattle said. "Although with risks involved obviously although Amelia did have training as a mid-wife as well through her nursing experience so it was certainly something she knew she was capable of doing. That was the beginning of a massive change in Amelia's life."

Dane moved her base of operations to the USA while Amelia took her "business plan" to heart. During this time, unmarried mothers did not have access to any kind of subsidy as the 1834 Poor Law Amendment Act did not oblige the fathers of illegitimate children to pay for their upbringing. These laws, coupled with the stigmatization of single mothers, forced the practice of baby farming.

Amelia discussed business strategies with Dane. She knew the best bet was to insist on being paid upfront with a one-time fee. She refused any type of money for continuous care as she knew that would mean the mother would return to visit.

"The one off premiums were certainly not enough to sustain a child's life for long financially," Vale said. "And the only way that it would be profitable for a baby farmer was to subject a child to persist underfeeding that would at some point bring about the infant's death."

"Abortion was not an option," Judith Knelman said. "So the simplest thing to do was hide, have the baby and get rid of it. Pay somebody to take care of it or pay somebody to get rid of it."

The babies were subsequently left on the premises and seen as "nurse children."

"Illegitimacy was seen as hugely immoral," said author Allison Rattle. "Even orphanages would only accept orphans from families where the parents were married and the father had died. They wouldn't accept a child who was born out of wedlock."

"Dickens did a really good job of describing social conditions in the 1850 and 60s," Knelman added. "Certainly there were a lot of poor people. There were a lot of neglected and abandoned children."

"There was no work," said Alan McCormick of Scotland Yard. "There was no social services. There was no welfare. One in every twelve women was a prostitute. A child being born in normal circumstances only had a fifty percent chance of reaching the age of five. So that's how bad it was."

BABY FARMING

"Baby farming was a business carried out throughout the country," said historian Ken Wells. "If a mother was unable to look after their child, there was an option of sending them out to a baby farmer, also known as fostering, with the understanding that they could visit the child whenever they wanted to."

On the surface they were providing a service to a growing need. They took an unwanted child and gave them to a foster parent. Only those foster parents and caregivers didn't always have the best interests of the infant at heart.

"MOTHER'S FRIEND"

The majority of these "caregivers" resorted to starving out the babies. They sedated crying babies with alcohol or drugs usually using Godfrey's Cordial, also known as 'Mother's Friend'. This syrup was one of the most popular medicines given to infants and children in both the United States and England in the latter years of the 18th and early 19th centuries. The syrup was used as a panacea to everything from colic to jaundice to excessive crying to diarrhea. 'Mother's Friend' was harmful despite its harmless sounding name as it contained one grain of opium for every two ounces. Many infants were poisoned from this syrup which was administered in secret by nurses who wanted to keep babies under their care in a deep state of sleep and thus more manageable.

"A hungry child, a noisy child, is a difficult child to raise," author Allison Vale said. "And something that was chillingly referred to colloquially as 'the Quietness' was an over the counter anti-colic cordial and it did contain liquid opium which was laudanum and in some cases brandy."

"People gave babies laudanum when they were supposed to be giving them food," Klansman said. "Because it dulled the need, or dulled the awareness of the baby that it was hungry. Of course it didn't nourish the baby so eventually a baby that was given that and not given enough food would die."

The babies would die from severe malnutrition but the coroner would record the death as "debility from birth", "lack of breast milk" or "starvation."

There were those guilt-ridden mothers who returned to the baby-farming homes to check on their children but would find their efforts blocked. Most would be too scared or embarrassed to inform the police of any wrongdoing. The police themselves had numerous problems tracking any children that were deemed missing.

"Dead infants," Vale said. "Or abandoned infants were as commonplace in British cities as roadkill today. Babies were found parceled up in railroad stations, under railroad arches."

"It was desperation," McCormick added. "For the vast majority of these ladies."

TO A MANNER BORN

With Dane's departure to the States, Amelia set her sights on taking her place in the baby-farming business. She had just given birth to her own daughter, Ellen, but in 1869 her husband George died.

A widow at age 32 with a baby, Amelia needed a new source of income...

She began taking in pregnant women as she placed ads to nurse and adopt the babies. In return, she required a large one-time fee and clothing for the child. She began meeting with expectant young women, convincing them that she was someone who could be trusted in providing a safe and loving home for their child.

Before she followed through with her plan, however, she put her own child up for adoption and sent her away.

"It was a choice that she made," Vale said. "She had options. She could have worked through. But instead what she does is to farm her own child out and opt for the easy money that she seemed to be able to make."

"As Amelia chose to go into the baby farming business," Rattle said. "She was maybe able to travel around here, there and everywhere adopting babies so it made sense for her daughter to be out of the way."

Three years after her first husband George died, Amelia remarried. His name was William Dyer, a brewers laborer from Bristol. They had two children together, Mary Ann aka Polly and William Samuel.

Amelia eventually left William, however, as the latter lost his job and offered little in the way of finances.

Strapped for cash, Amelia decided to dispense with the heavy cost of letting the babies die through neglect and starvation. So after each child was born she promptly murdered them, thus incurring a windfall of profits.

"Baby farmers used different methods," Klansman said. "Some of which are less palatable than others."

"Quite often she would suffocate babies at birth," Rattle said. "Smothering the baby the moment its head came out, before it turned blue as that would be a sign that it had taken its first breath. (She made) it would look like a stillbirth so the death certificate would all be above board."

When her daughter Polly asked why so many babies came and disappeared, Amelia described herself as the "angel maker."

"I'm sending little children to Jesus," Amelia said. "Because he wanted them far more than their mothers did."

"Cold," Alan McCormick of New Scotland Yard said in describing Amelia. "Those kids meant nothing to her. It was just a means of getting money."

It can be argued, however, that once Amelia got a taste of killing she did it more for the power than the money and greed.

"The actual killing of the child," Holmes said. "Watching the child peacefully to some degree die. It parallels perhaps seeing her mother pass away where she felt an almost God-like power over these children that she had decided were going to go to their maker."

AROUSING SUSPICION

"Amelia was already aware of the fact that this was not going to be about her helping children," forensic psychologist David Holmes said. "This was going to be a fairly cruel and anti-mothering act that would be carried out in order to gain all of this money."

Amelia successfully avoided police involvement until 1879, a good ten years into her murderous ways. A doctor became suspicious about the number of child deaths he had been called in to certify under Amelia's care.

"The inquests were held in Somerset," Vale said. "And they're (the police) pretty certain that the babies have died as a direct result of neglect and opium overdose. But they can't prove it. And interestingly, she gets off with a six months sentence with hard labor."

Without a coroner that was able to rule completely against her, Amelia would have undoubtedly been executed by hanging.

"Its incredibly really," Rattle said. "That she only got six months. And there was one example, we read of a chap who got twelve months for stealing a piece of bacon."

Amelia took the punishment hard, becoming an emotional wreck during her jail stay. She resumed her business, however, as soon as she was released.

"In the long term," Holmes reasoned. "It mostly would have served as a very hard lesson in forensic awareness that she wasn't gonna get caught again. And there was no way she was going to leave any evidence which had been the problem in leading up to her capture."

She was sent to mental hospitals for supposed mental illness and suicidal ideations but these seemed to be well-timed acts. From her experience of working in an asylum, Amelia knew the tricks of the trade in order to make her stay an easy one.

"I don't think Amelia Dyer was insane," said Vale. "I think she was a very bad person who deliberately committed murder for profit."

Amelia had both an alcohol and substance abuse problem, using on a regular basis as she began her killings once again.

"Certainly the drugs would have had an impact on her," Richards said. "On her mental state. Maybe induced this complete detachment from reality."

"A long term laudanum habit," Vale concurred. "Will lead to periods of depression. It can lead to mood swings even when you're not under the influence. I think it also exacerbates any underlying mental health issues."

RETURNING TO BABY FARMING

In 1884, British society took a much harder line against baby farming and any sign of neglect or abuse would be reported.

"She definitely changes her modus operandi at this point (after 1884)," Vale said. "She's beginning to murder these children."

In 1890, Amelia took on the care of the illegitimate baby of a governess. She had begun targeting the babies of the more affluent because of the larger amounts of money involved. The higher up the social class the woman was, however, the more risk was involved as the woman may have means to question and come after Amelia.

"This was a young governess who fell in love with the young master of the house that she worked in and had got pregnant," Rattle said. "She was left on her own and she responds to an advert, gets in touch with Amelia Dyer and moves in with her. Amelia was able to gain the trust of this woman as with many others, so much so that the governess was persuaded to leave her baby in the care of Amelia once it was born."

The governess, however, returned to visit her baby months later and immediately became suspicious that the child she was given was not hers. She stripped the baby to see if a birth mark was present on one of its hips. It wasn't and the governess immediately informed the authorities.

The police, however, could never pin Amelia down.

"She managed to put them off time and time again by sending them on wild goose chases," Rattle said. "She said she had sent them to a couple that moved here...that moved there."

Amelia continued to move from town to town but still found herself being stalked by the governess who wouldn't give up.

"She did feel hounded," Richards said. "I'm sure that would have had an impact on her. She would have felt that pressure."

Amelia then feigned another nervous breakdown and a doctor was brought in. "The birds are telling me to do it! The birds are telling me to do it!" she would cry out, forcing the doctor to send her to an asylum.

"She was a very clever lady," Holmes said. "With the police getting close to her and she needed to lose herself and what better place to go than somewhere like that (a mental asylum)."

Her mental illness continued on unabated as she drank two bottles of laudanum in an attempted suicide. Her long term use of opium, however, allowed her to build up the tolerance necessary to survive.

"Amelia would be drawn to the idea of self-medicating," Holmes said. "Possibly seeing it as a route, a means to ease the situation, make it even easier for her to put up with what she was doing."

"She took it (opium) on a regular basis," Richards said. "She took it almost daily so she was an addict. So that would induce a form of state from her mentally where she would be detached from reality and I think that was part of her coping mechanism to detach from the reality of what she was doing."

After that close call and subsequent hospital release, Amelia resumed baby farming and murder.

"Her mental breakdowns were very short lived," Richards noted. "She would be out of sorts for a period of time that get it all back together again. To me that would say there isn't a mental illness there."

A CLEVER KILLER

She wised up to doing things on the books and decided to stop getting doctors to issue death certificates. Amelia decided to kill and bury the bodies herself. In order to do this, she would have to be a killer on the run as inevitably the mothers would come back seeking to reclaim their children or check on their welfare. Amelia took her family to different cities to escape suspicion as soon as things got too hot. She would use a series of different aliases and rename her businesses.

"Amelia committed what many serial killers do," Holmes explained. "The mistake of accelerating and being over enthusiastic. Either for reasons that she was enjoying the process or quite simply greed was driving her over the edge."

Baby farming began to gain the attention and compassion of the British ruling class, however. They asked why if they had laws for the prevention of the cruelty of animals then why didn't there laws protecting children. With the arrest and hanging of Margaret Waters (another baby farming killer) and the fleeing Dyer, Amelia's colleagues were going downhill fast and perhaps she thought her time was limited.

By 1893, Amelia had another breakdown but was released from the Wells mental asylum. This would be the last time she would be hospitalized. She moved to Caversham, Berkshire with a woman named Jane "Granny" Smith who didn't know of Amelia's exploits.

"She befriends an old lady named Jane Smith," Vale said. "She's widowed and resigned to spend her last days in the workhouse. Amelia seduces her with stories of rescuing the unwanted infants. Of nursing them. And it's a very, very seductive image. And Jane Smith buys into it, wholesale."

Her daughter Mary Ann aka Polly and her husband Arthur Palmer came along as well.

The group moved to 45 Kensington Road, Reading Berkshire in that same year. Amelia had the perfect front. She coached Jane Smith to call her "mother" in front of prospective clients while Amelia would call her "Granny."

A ruse to project a mother-daughter image and put the guards down of the pregnant young women.

"Jane Smith didn't get the life she was promised at all," Rattle said. "She was treated as no more than a servant really. She was made to look after the children, to clean the house."

Amelia then puts her adoptions into overdrive. The babies come in and out of the house with such rapidity that old lady Jane Smith doesn't even learn their names.

Eyewitnesses later claimed that there were six infants a day coming to and from the house daily.

THE MURDERS CONTINUE

The advertisement in the "Miscellaneous" column of the Bristol Times & Mirror newspaper was poignant.

In January of 1896 a popular barmaid named Evelina Marmon gave birth to a daughter out of wedlock. She named the baby Doris and she sought immediately to have it adopted. She placed an ad in the "Miscellaneous" section of the Bristol Times & Mirror newspaper.

"Wanted, respectable woman to take young child." Marmon intended to go back to work and hoped to eventually reclaim her child.

Evelina was a God-fearing farmer's daughter who left the farm for city life. She found work as a barmaid in the saloon of the Plough Hotel, an old coaching inn. She was buxom with blonde hair and had a vibrant personality. She had plenty of suitors and became pregnant by one of the male patrons who left her deserted.

Evelina knew she could not bring up the baby on her own.

She would have to find a foster home for little Doris - to have her "adopted out", in the language of the time - go back to work and hope in time to be able to reclaim her child.

Next to her own ad was an advertisement that read *"Married couple with no family would adopt healthy child, nice country home. Terms, £10".*

Marmon answered the ad which was addressed to a "Mrs. Harding", an alias of Amelia. A few days later Amelia wrote back, saying *"I should be glad to have a dear little baby girl, one I could bring up and call my own. We are plain, homely people, in fairly good circumstances. I don't want a child for money's sake, but for company and home comfort... Myself and my husband are dearly fond of children. I have no child of my own. A child with me will have a good home and a mother's love. It is just lovely here, heatlhy and pleasant. There is an orchard opposite our front door."*

Evelina was assured that she could visit whenever she wished.

"Rest assured I will do my duty by that dear child. I will be a mother, as far as lies in my power."

"It is just lovely here, healthy and pleasant. There is an orchard opposite our front door."

Evelina tried to negotiate a weekly fee for the care of Doris but Amelia wanted a substantial one-time fee to be paid upfront. Evelina, seemingly with no other choice, agreed to pay the £10, and a week later "Mrs Harding" arrived in Cheltenham.

Evelina was surprised that Amelia aka "Mrs. Harding" was old (59 years) and heavy set (over 210 lbs). She remained reluctant at first but gave in as the elderly woman immediately showed her Doris some affection, covering her with a shawl.

Evelina gave the old lady a cardboard box of clothes she had prepared – nappies, chemises, petticoats, frocks, nightgowns, and a powder box. She also enclosed the money and received a signed receipt from "Mrs.Harding."

She accompanied her baby daughter and her eventual killer to Cheltenham station then on to Gloucester. Evelina stood there crying through the hot steam on the platform as the 5:20 p.m train took her baby away.

When Evelina returned home, she described herself as "a broken woman."

Days later, she received a letter from "Mrs. Harding" offering her assurance that all was well with her daughter. Evelina wrote back but received no replies afterward.

Amelia told Evelina that she would be going to Reading but lied. She traveled to 76 Mayo Road, Willesden, London where her daughter Mary Ann was staying. Amelia then took some white edging tape and wrapped it around the baby's neck, making a strangling knot. The baby did not die immediately.

"I used to like to watch them with the tape around their neck," Amanda said. "But it was soon all over with them."

"The idea of strangling and using the tape may make it seem almost symbolical or bizarre to ourselves," Holmes said. "But in terms of criminal awareness she was aware of the fact that if she tried to suffocate a baby its not always absolutely certain that the baby is dead."

The mother and daughter team wrapped the baby up with a napkin. They kept the clothes that Evelina gave her and hoped to sell it to a pawnbroker. Amelia used some of the money to pay the rent to her landlady and gave the woman a pair of child's boots as a present for her own little girl.

The following day, April 1st of 1896, a young boy named Harry Simmons was taken to the Mayo Road residence. Amelia had no spare white edging tape available and used the tape from Doris' corpse to strangle the year old boy.

The next day both bodies were rolled into a carpet bag, their corpses stacked one on top of the other. Bricks were added inside for additional weight. Amelia headed back toward Reading, taking the bus to Paddington and then the train. She dragged the carpet bag through the streets until she reached the River Thames. She had a secluded spot at Caversham Lock and she forced the carpet bag through the railing and didn't leave until she heard it splash into the waters below.

She didn't know she had a witness as a man passed, hurrying on his way home calling out "Good night."

A SHOCKING DISCOVERY

Ironically, only days before the dumping of the bodies a package was fished out of the Thames by a bargeman. This package was the work of Amelia as she had not weighed it down adequately. It contained the body of a baby girl named Helena Fry. With only a small police force available in Reading, a Constable Anderson made a significant discovery. He found a label from Temple Meads Station, Bristol and he used microscopic analysis of the wrapping paper. He found a faintly legible name. A "Mrs. Thomas" and an address.

The address of Amelia Dyer.

The police immediately placed Amelia's home under surveillance. They did enough research on Amelia and knew that she would "disappear" if she thought she was under suspicion. So they decided they would be better served if they would use a young woman as a decoy to secure a meeting with Amelia and discuss the prospect of using her "adoptive services."

On April 3rd, while Amelia was waiting on the decoy to arrive, she answered the door to a police raid. The smell of decomposing bodies radiated throughout her home but no human remains were found. The police found other evidence, however, such as the white edging tape, telegrams describing adoption arrangements, pawn tickets for children's clothing, receipts for newspaper ads and letters from distraught mothers asking about the welfare of their child.

The police determined that in the few months Amelia had been in Reading at least twenty children had been placed into her care. She had been preparing to move again, this time to the town of Somerset.

Amelia was arrested on April 4th, three days after the murders of Doris Marmon and Harry Simmons. The Thames River was searched and six more bodies were discovered, including Doris and Harry.

Each child had been strangled with the seamstress white tape and Amelia later told police that "was how you could tell it was one of mine."

Eleven days later, Evelina Marmon had been contacted by police as they found her name in items found in Amelia's home. Distraught, she came to identify her daughter's remains.

THE TRIAL OF A KILLER

An inquest was held a month later. Amelia's daughter Mary Ann and her husband Arthur were not charged as there was no direct evidence that they were her accomplices. Arthur was set free because of a confession handwritten by Amelia. She wrote:

Sir will you kindly grant me the favour of presenting this to the magistrates on Saturday the 18th instant I have made this statement out, for I may not have the opportunity then I must relieve my mind I do know and I feel my days are numbered on this earth but I do feel it is an awful thing drawing innocent people into trouble I do know I shal have to answer before my Maker in Heaven for the awful crimes I have committed but as God Almighty is my judge in Heaven a on Hearth neither my daughter Mary Ann Palmer nor her husband Alfred Ernest Palmer I do most solemnly declare neither of them had any thing at all to do with it, they never knew I contemplated doing such a wicked thing until it was to late I am speaking the truth and nothing but the truth as I hope to be forgiven, I myself and I alone must stand before my Maker in Heaven to give an answer for it all witnes my hand

Amelia Dyer.

—April 16, 1896

On May 22nd, 1896, Amelia appeared in court and pleaded guilty to the murder of Doris Marmon. Her family and friends testified that they had their own suspicions about Amelia and spoke of times that she evaded discovery. A man came forth claiming he had seen and spoken to Amelia as she had disposed of two bodies at Caversham Lock proved key to the prosecution.

Amelia used insanity as a defense, offering her stays in mental asylums as proof of her instability. The prosecution, however, argued that her symptoms were well-rehearsed actions to avoid suspicion as both of her hospital stays coincided with times that Amelia felt her murders would be discovered.

The jury took four and a half minutes to find her guilty. Amelia then spent three weeks in her condemned cell, filling five journals with her confessions. A chaplain visited her the night before her execution and asked if she had anything to confess. She offered him her journals, asking "isn't this enough?"

Amelia was then subpoenaed to appear as a witness in her daughter's own trial for murder which was set for a week after her own execution date. The court ruled, however, that Amelia became "legally dead" after she was sentenced and her testimony would be inadmissible.

On the day of her execution, Amelia discovered that the charges against her daughter had been dropped.

On June 10th, 1896, Amelia Dyer was hanged by James Billington at Newgate Prison. Asked on the scaffold if she had anything to say, she said "I have nothing to say."

URBAN LEGEND?

It remains unknown as to why Amelia's daughter Mary Ann aka Polly was never convicted. Her own daughter provided the majority of the testimony that procured the conviction of her mother but nothing is said about her own involvement.

And the baby murders did not stop after Amelia's death.

Two years after her execution, railroad workers inspecting carriages found a parcel tied up with a string inside a siding on the Plymouth express.

Inside was a three-week old baby girl. The infant was shivering and wet...but alive.

A little research showed that the baby was the child of a widow named Jane Hill. Hill had given the baby to a woman named "Mrs. Stewart" for the one time fee of £12.

"The little one would have a good home and a parent's love and care," Mrs. Stewart had written, her prose eerilly echoing that of Amelia Dyer. "Mrs. Stewart" had picked up the baby at Plymouth and dumped her on the next train.

The conjecture was that "Mrs. Stewart" was none other than Polly, Amelia's daughter.

MARSHA MAREK & OTHER FEMALE SERIAL KILLERS

51

PETE DOVE

Marsh Marek – The Viennese Poisoner

Vienna is one of the world's most beautiful cities. Its architecture is without precedent. Whether taking in the breath-taking views from the giddying heights of St Stephen's Cathedral, or admiring the turrets and towers of the City Hall, Vienna is a feast for the eyes.

And the stomach. Little on Earth beats sitting at a street side table in some Viennese café, rich coffee in front and the velvet taste of sumptuous Sache Torte scintillating the taste buds. It seems almost sacrilegious to remind ourselves that some of Austria's past leaves the bitter taste of dubious morality.

The nation – or its leaders at least – had put up little resistance to Hitler's annexation of the country in early 1938. In fact, the rampant Nazi party in the landlocked country had welcomed the Fascist regime with open arms.

Indeed, Hitler was so confident of a cheery welcome that he accompanied his troops as they marched into Austria, and received the kind of greeting normally reserved for heroes rather than conquering leaders. Not every citizen was pleased to see the neighbours march through the door, however. Particularly so the Jewish community in Austria, along with those from the Romany population, patients who suffered from mental illness and the hidden homosexual inhabitants.

Martha Marek was another who would soon be looking on the invaders with a jaundiced eye. As somebody considered half Jewish, she would already have plenty to worry about. But, as we will see, Adolf Hitler was about to play a significant role in her ultimate and, many would argue, deserved demise.

Martha was born into almost as unpleasant circumstances as those in which she would later die. She was born and very quickly abandoned. Unsurprisingly, under these circumstances, there is a lot of uncertainty around her early years. Even the year and place of her birth are reported variously. Some accounts list her birth date and place as 1904 in Vienna; others report her as entering the world at the turn of the century. Still more identify her place of birth as Sopron, which is in Hungary. The safest conclusion is that she was born somewhere in central Europe during the early years of the twentieth century,

What happened next is equally unclear. The most probable explanation of her earliest years is that she spent a few months with her mother – her biological father is unknown – before being fostered by a kindly couple, a chef and his wife.

However, while still a toddler, her real mother married Rudolph Lowenstein, who was the station master in the town of Baden, close to the Austrian capital. Young Martha was then able to re-join her mother. However, playing happy families was just not to be for the Lowenstein clan. By the time Martha was seven, the station master had bought a one way ticket to America – alone. Once more, Martha's mother felt that she could not cope with a small child, and the girl found herself this time living in a charity home in Vienna.

She re-joined her mother again at twelve, and earned some pennies running errands for a dress shop. Then, when she was around the age of thirteen, Martha's life took a significant and twisted turn.

Once again, exact details are sketchy – many of them based on Martha's own, somewhat selective, memories. Moritz Fritsch was a wealthy department store owner whose expensive shop occupied a place in the heart of Vienna's downtown. The time in question was, according to Martha, set in the years leading up to the World War. Fritsch was already sixty two when he first set eyes on the child, waif like and hungry looking, as she travelled on a streetcar.

He was immediately fascinated by the young girl; he engaged her in conversation and indicated that as she had experience working in a dress shop, he might be able to find her better paid employment in his own store. It takes little reading between the lines to at least suspect that Fritsch's intentions were not exactly noble.

He contacted the young girl's mother and very soon she was ensconced in his luxurious villa in the wealthy Moedling district of

Vienna. Martha became officially listed as his ward. Depending on her actual age when she entered his home, the claims of what happened next fit somewhere between the rather uncomfortable and the downright illegal. It is alleged that Fritsch saw in his young ward more than the chance to do good and offer the down at heel girl (and, later, her half sister whom he also adopted) the best education money could buy. Instead, his interest was, at least in part, sexual. Or so some investigators into Martha Marek's life are keen to claim. Other, kinder, commentators describe the magnate as 'hearty' and 'generous'.

Whichever is the truer take, certainly, his own son and daughter were sufficiently unimpressed by the new arrangements that they moved out of the house, and went instead to live with their mother, whom Fritsch had divorced in 1900.

Although getting on in years, Fritsch was a healthy and energetic man, and his death at the age of 74 was something a surprise. A suspicious one. Rumours were bandied about that the wealthy department store owner had been helped on his way with poison.

The allegation was hard to prove. Neither his son or daughter were keen to have their father's body exhumed and examined. Scandal would certainly follow such a move and that would be harmful for business. In any case, although their inheritance was less than it might have been, they still became very wealthy young people when their father's will was enacted.

So, too, did his young ward. From penniless urchin, by the time she was in her early twenties Martha was a rich girl in her own right. She intended to enjoy her new-found status. Within three months of her lover's death, Martha was married. Her husband was a student, Emil Marek, who was studying at the Vienna Technical Institute. Unusually for the time, Emil married an older woman – just - Martha being just three years his senior.

The extent to which he was in love is uncertain. He could have just been bowled over by the attentions of a woman who would have seemed a wealthy sophisticate in his eyes. More certain is that Emil was not the strongest character. He was so embarrassed at having a wife older than he that he immediately left his studies, and grew a wispy beard in the hope that it might make him seem more mature.

While at his college, Emil's subject had been engineering. With money behind him, albeit his wife's, he set about launching unworkable scheme after unlikely engineering project. One of these was the electrification of Burgenland, which was Austria's least technically advanced province. Astonishingly, the inexperienced, young and failed student persuaded the Government to match the money he was prepared to put into the project. Sensing that he and Martha were about to turn from the category of very comfortably off to the exclusive club of the super rich, he took the forward thinking step of insuring his life. No doubt, under the encouragement of his wife.

It was a decision he would come to regret.

He took out the insurance with the Anglo-Danubian Lloyd Company, which was based in Vienna. In the even of his death, his wife would receive a hearty sum equivalent in today's money of $100000. Even more impressively, permanent disability would earn him four times that amount. His first premium was made on June 11th 1925.

Clearly, the decision to start the policy from that date was fortuitous. Very, very fortuitous. Because on the exact next day, June 12th 1925, the following unfortunate incident occurred: Emil was working at home, in the garden of the Moedling Villa he shared with Martha. He was chopping a block of wood when the razor sharp tool slipped. A scream burst from his lips, one no doubt muffled by his bravery, but sufficient to attract Martha and Paula, her half-sister. They emerged to see Emil lying prostrate, blood pouring from his leg. This, in turn, was dangling almost in two, the halves connected by no more than a sinew. Stoically, Martha called the doctor who, seeing that the leg was impossible to save, promptly cut it off.

We know that this is the order of events because it is what Martha and Emil told the insurance company, their story so neatly put together it must have been true. Surely. Who could doubt it? For the insurers Emil's accident was about to prove costly. A nasty accident led to permanent disability. $400000 please.

Unsurprisingly, the Anglo-Danubian Insurance Company was more than a tad suspicious. They travelled to the Moedling hospital and examined the leg. It appeared as though Emil was even braver than suspected. Remarkably, it appeared, he had continued with his chopping even after the first blow fell into his lower limb. In fact, the same thing had happened twice more. The leg showed evidence of three separate blows.

But then the intrigue deepened. Karl Mraz had been an orderly at the hospital, and he would be happy to tell any trial that there was more to the savaged leg than met the eye. That was because, he would testify, he had overheard doctors discussing that the insurance company was paying them to 'fix' the leg so it appeared as though it had been struck three times. That Mraz was being paid by the Mareks to give this testimony was conveniently omitted from his evidence. Further, the fact that Mraz was also observed entering and leaving the Marek's villa was, of course, purely coincidental...if rather inconvenient to the defense.

The couple were arrested, but when the matter came to court it found in their favour. Partly. The court decided the couple were not guilty of defrauding their insurers, but they did receive a small sentence each for their involvement with Mraz's lies. However, they had already been held in custody and much to public joy – the couple were front page news and generally seen as young heroes against the wicked insurance company – were immediately released. In the end, the insurance company settled for about the equivalent of $50000 in Austrian marks, much of which was used by the Marek's to pay their legal costs.

But if luck was with them at that time, it soon went away. Or, perhaps more accurately, the couple's atrocious business plans contributed to their change in fortune. Fritsch's money was long gone, wasted on good living and bad ideas, and the insurance monies quickly followed. Among the more ludicrous plans of the impractical young couple were a taxi fleet that quickly drove itself out of business; a plan to build utilities in North Africa that sent their monies rapidly down the drain and a planned vegetable market that harvested nothing.

During these tough times family life deteriorated. Martha began to hate her failure of a husband, a man whose ideas were only matched in their frailty by his health. The couple did manage two children in that time, Alfons was born in 1929 and Ingeborg came along three years later. But their money was gone, and they sold the villa to pay off debts and moved to a far less salubrious part of the city.

In fact, money was so tight that Emil returned part time to his parents, taking meals with them and, remarkably, gaining health. It was only when he returned to his wife that illness returned. This time, with a vengeance. Within a month, his eyesight had failed and the invalid lost weight with astonishing rapidity. He was admitted to hospital, where he died on July 31st 1932. His death certificate listed tuberculosis as the cause of his passing.

Martha really did seem feted to the most unfortunate, luckless spell. Or her family did. Within a few weeks of her husband's death, young Ingeborg became ill. As if often the case with a small child, the cause of her sickness was very difficult for doctors to pinpoint. All that they knew was she went downhill fast, and tragically on September 2nd of the same year her father died, so did she. Just one month and two days passed between the deaths of Martha's husband and her daughter.

Fortunately for the grieving woman, the pain of her husband's and daughter's terrible deaths were eased a little. Both had been insured, and each bereavement earned her a pay-out. At least the young woman could stop peddling vegetables on the streets. At least she could spend more time being a caring mother to her remaining child.

Astonishingly, or not as it turns out, Alfons was the next to fall ill. It seemed as though some terrible canker was attacking the family one by one. Of course, that was true, although the it was a disease from within the home that was causing all of the danger and destruction. Still the authorities suspected nothing. Perhaps the root of their failure to act lay in Martha herself. She was young, attractive and even though she might not be the socialite she once was, there was a residue of glamour attached to her. Relatively recently she had been the public's pin up girl, the woman who successfully took on that most hated of institutions, an insurance company. It was inconceivable that the misfortune striking her family down was the result of her own actions.

This time, there was some good news. Alfons' illness was caught quickly enough by doctors. Probably more by chance than good medicine, whatever treatments they offered him worked. His decline was halted and the young boy steadily recovered from the mysterious ailment that had afflicted him. Of course, with hindsight it is quite reasonably to draw the conclusion that Alfons' life was saved simply because he was hospitalized and was therefore away from his mother. Healthy, unadulterated food allied to the good fortune of having been hospitalized before irreparable damage had been done were the reasons that he survived.

Matters settled down. For eighteen months nothing untoward attacked the Marek family. Martha began to look further afield for the chance to find some funds, and discovered that a distant Aunt – elderly, mostly neglected and, crucially, reasonably well off – had turned into a lonely old woman. Suzanne Lowenstein was sixty seven, and her marriage to a member of the Lowenstein brood brought her under Martha's radar. That uncle had been an army surgeon but had died, leaving his wife with a tidy sum.

Martha began to take an interest in the elderly Aunt. She was a skilled manipulator of people, as able to charm an elderly woman as easily as she could lure a man into her bedroom. Aunt Suzanne was delighted by the interest shown by her debonair young niece, a lady who appeared to have herself fallen so unfortunately on hard times.

Indeed, it made total sense for the poor unfortunate to move into her rambling home, and act as a friendly, live in, companion to her. In fact, she was so flattered by the attentions she received that she decided it was time to re-write her will. The elderly lady instructed her lawyer to make Martha Marek, caring niece and victim of life's unpredictable slings and arrows, her main beneficiary. In fact, her sole beneficiary.

That was in the summer of 1934. In June she had begun to show symptoms of some kind of vague illness. In the beginning of July the will was changed, and Aunt Suzanne started to go properly downhill. Her sight deteriorated rapidly. Her mobility faltered, and soon she was bed-ridden. Her hair began to fall out by the handful, and her eyesight failed. Her decline from slightly dotty, but active, Aunt to invalid was astonishingly fast. Whatever illness had afflicted her, doctors concluded, must be virulent indeed. So virulent, in fact, that on July 17th she died.

Still, the blow to Martha was eased a little. She had the inheritance her Aunt had left. She could remain in the comfortably rented apartment her Aunt had lived in, and enjoy the expensive furnishings willed to her. And thanks to her usual resilience in the face of tragedy, her period of mourning was short. Very quickly, Martha was spending lavishly once more. Her aunt's money would not last her for long.

Jeno Neumann was an insurance salesman who had the misfortune to become acquainted with Martha. Although, at forty nine, he was a good deal older than the would be socialite, as with most men she was able to both manipulate him, and dominate him. He moved into the luxurious home and became a sub tenant, and then the latest in a long line of lovers Martha enjoyed.

Being involved in insurance was a handy attribute as far as Martha was concerned. Cynics might even suggest that this experience made Neumann a more attractive proposition than any good looks or witty mind he might possess. (These is no evidence that the poor man benefitted from either of these characteristics.)

Martha decided to let another room in the house, and advertised for a tenant. After an appropriate period of due diligence with regards to applicants, she settled on a fifty three year old seamstress, Felicitas Kittenberger, to become her lodger. At the same time as offering a room, she was also able to reassure Mrs Kittenberger that, thanks to her many wealthy friends and associates, there would be plenty of work heading her way.

The next stage of her scheme was to persuade Neumann to issue an insurance policy for Mrs Kittenberger; and, as landlord Martha Marek was named as the bearer in the event that the tenant should have the misfortune to become deceased. Remarkably, she quickly became ill. The poor tenant lost the use of her legs; her eyes began to fail and each morning her pillow would be littered with locks of hair. On June 2nd 1934 the unfortunate seamstress died. Once more, the shock for Martha was alleviated by an insurance pay-out of, after taxes, the equivalent (in contemporary money) of just under $800.

But if Martha was not overly distressed by the outcome, the same could not be said for Mrs Kittenberger's son, Herbert. He confronted his mother's landlady, and accused her of murder. With remarkable composure, Martha simply called the police and had him arrested, although in the circumstances he was let off with a warning and sent on his way.

Events in the Marek household went remarkably quiet for a couple of years. Then, in October 1936, Martha attempted a different money raising scheme. In some ways, it was the least harmful of all her methods of getting cash. It did not involve her hacking off her husband's leg with an axe. Nobody was killed. But it did lead to her downfall.

Inspector of the Vienna police Rudolph Peternell had no idea that he was about to become involved in one of the most infamous crimes in Austrian history (Nazism aside). On October 31st 1936 he headed out to a comfortable part of the city in order to speak to the victim of a burglary. The woman he saw at the somewhat overbearing apartment made an immediate impression. Flame haired and attractive in a manicured, sophisticated way, she was also suffering from some obvious recent illness. She limped around the apartment, using her hands to feel her way. One hand, in fact, because the other hung limply by her side.

The reason for her struggles were, the lady told the inspector, that she was recovering from a recent stroke. Both her sight and her mobility had been affected.

Peternell set to work with a standard array of questions. Mrs Marek had, she told the officer, sent her maid home early the previous night as the young girl wished to see a movie. Then, she had retired to bed at her usual time with nothing amiss. The next day, however, Mrs Marek had realised there was something very wrong indeed.

'In the morning,' she said, her voice frail sounding, 'on entering the drawing room, I soon discovered that certain articles were missing. Not only tapestries and paintings, but jewellery.'

Peternell asked whether there had been aware of anything unusual during the night. Her answer seemed, on the face of it, plausible.

'Ever since suffering a stroke,' she explained as a reason for hearing nothing of the burglary, 'I have been a very heavy sleeper.'

The conversation moved on until it reached the tricky question of the extent of the robbery. Martha Marek told the officer that property worth about two and a half thousand dollars (or the equivalent in Austrian marks) had been lost. On questioning, she confirmed that she had insurance which covered almost the entire amount.

Peternell made a list of the missing articles, and headed back to the station. It was while he was travelling to his headquarters that a couple of questions sprung to his mind. Even by the end of 1936, Martha Marek enjoyed a kind of limited local notoriety – everyone loves a poor girl made good. He recalled reading recently that she had been seen at a party in a local dance hall. He recalled no mention made of any ill health, and thought it odd that a woman so apparently disabled should attend such a party, and even odder that, having done so, reporters had not picked up on the human interest story of her physical decline. Strange.

Then he thought back to the itinerary he had made of missing items. Tapestries are large, heavy and easily identified. In fact, exactly the sort of thing a thief would avoid unless stealing to order. On the other hand, the apartment had been littered with valuable looking pieces of silver – items easily transportable and simple to sell on. Peternell reported his doubts to his superiors. They listened, and decided to look into Martha Marek's file...if she had one. They soon realised that she did indeed have a dossier of past incidents. An extremely bulky one. Martha Marek was, they decided, a woman worth keeping a close eye on.

Peternell and a colleague, Josef Gunacker, were charged with maintaining a watch on their subject. And with making enquiries.

One of the most remarkable things about Martha Marek was that she got away with things for so long. It is amazing what a careful back story, good looks and a bit of luck can achieve, because what was for certain was that she was not a great criminal.

The detectives spoke to the janitor of the block where she lived, and he reported seeing her moving a number of large bundles to a truck on the evening of October 31st, the night her robbery was supposed to have occurred. To the janitor, she seemed in her normal state of good health. The notion that she was suffering the after-effects of a stroke were an embroidery of her story which was neither thought through, nor sustainable.

The detectives hunted out the storage warehouse where Martha's bundles had been delivered on the night of October 31st. They were, unsurprisingly, the very ones she had reported as being stolen.

Next Peternell persuaded Martha's cleaning lady to lie to her mistress. In return for a handy sum, she told Martha that, on a particular day, she would be unable to attend but would send a substitute cleaner instead. The lady who turned up worked for the police, and soon confirmed that Martha was as healthy as she.

Clear in their minds that Martha's report of having been burgled was no more than a fraudulent attempt to get some insurance money, they turned their attentions to the more serious matters of the oddly high number of people who met a premature end after they became close to Martha Marek. The bodies of her husband Emil, her daughter Ingeborg, he aunt and lodger were exhumed. An investigation, even one as primitive as those that were used pre-war,` indicated a large quantity of the chemical thallium present in the corpses. This is often used as a rat poison. Investigations suggested that Martha Marek must have a long standing problem with rats, wherever she was living, because she was a regular purchaser of the product.

She was arrested, and her trial began on May 2nd 1938. It was to be a spectacular affair. In Austria at the time capital punishment was available to the courts and employed the especially gruesome method of beheading by guillotine. Confessing to her crimes would undoubtedly have led to the 'Devil in Petticoats', as she was dubbed in the popular press, escaping such a fate. But, despite the many efforts of the prosecutor to inveigle a confession from her, Martha would do no such thing. Indeed, such was the venom with which she stared at the attorney that on one occasion he told her: 'Don't try to hypnotize me madam!'

Indeed, Martha seemed determined to turn the whole trial into a fiasco. At one point she told the prosecutor: 'I wish you would be as good a father as I am a mother.' Even the judge did not escape her ire. 'You know more about stealing than I do,' she told him after he asked about a theft.

But her protests were in vain. The prosecution had over fourteen hundred pages of evidence and a hundred witnesses. Crucial among them were the detectives variously hired by insurance companies she had defrauded. Another, a pharmacist, reported selling her so much rat poison that he had had to increase his wholesale supply.

Still, when the inevitable verdict of guilt was cast, and Martha was sentenced to death, nobody thought it would happen. No woman had been executed in Austria for thirty years, none in Vienna for sixty. But they had not counted on Hitler becoming involved. He had his own executioner in his employ, and was determined that a hard line must be followed.

Johann Reichart killed more than 3000 people in his role as Hitler's leading criminal executioner. Martha Marek would prove to be one of the more challenging of his career. As she awaited her fate, once more she claimed to have lost use of her legs, but Reichart was a professional. His team practised tipping a wheelchair until its occupant fell straight onto the guillotine block.

As she was wheeled from her cell, by some kind of miracle Martha regained her mobility and fought fiercely against the violent fate awaiting her. She even managed to hit the cold eyed superstar executioner with a sharp kick. But she was overpowered, thrown onto the guillotine and, struggling until the last, despatched with one sharp fall of the blade.

There is a more than a touch of the macabre about the case of Martha Marek, even down to her alliterative name. She could easily feature in a late night Hallowe'en drama, one aiming to raise as many laughs as screams. Her inability to chop off her husband's leg in one blow, her pathetic attempts to appear disabled from a stroke, even her bizarre outbursts at her trial, all seem more at home in the pages of second rate fiction than the records of a capital court.

But we should not forget that she was a callous killer, one who murdered people she knew for personal greed. Included in her catalogue of victims, of course, are not only her husband but her baby daughter as well. As far as we know, only one of her intended victims survived: her son, Alfons. At Martha's trial a witness, neighbour Eugenie Hellinger, put the evil of Martha Marek into perspective. She told the court that Alfons had said the following to her, one day, before being rescued from his own poisoning.

'I shall soon go to Heaven,' he told the neighbor. 'My mother told me so.'

JILL ROCKCASTLE

Sarah Thompson

JILL ROCKCASTLE

For some, gambling is a special treat - a past-time for birthdays, anniversaries and celebrations. It can be a bonding experience that brings everyone together through either luck, or misfortune. For others, gambling becomes an addiction, where they are willing to lie, cheat and steal in order to get their fix. For the lucky few, gambling can become a lifestyle. This lifestyle is often fraught with drugs, danger, embezzlement, lies and fraud. Like many of the stories that have come before them, the story of Bill Gustafik and Jill Rockcastle is one that would make any big-screenwriter proud. When you put in all the ingredients of drugs, grand theft, a professional poker player, a murder and an attempt at suicide, you get something that sounds so surreal, no one could have lived through it.

The truth is, Jill Rockcastle did live through it - but her husband, tragically, did not. While one's heart may feel the instinctive pull to go out to Jill, the reality is much worse. The story of Bill and Jill is set in Las Vegas, where gambling, drugs and danger go hand-in-hand. In the early morning hours of April 13th in 2007, police received an anonymous tip about a dead body on the 23rd floor of a condominium building. This was only the beginning of a web that would slowly begin to unravel, and make it clear that the story of Jill Rockcastle is almost indistinguishable from the story of Bill Gustafik - you cannot tell one story without the other. They're inseparable, even after death.

Jill Rockcastle and Bill Gustafik seemed like a couple who couldn't be happier. Jill and Bill met not long after Bill had divorced his previous wife in 2000. He had also graduated from chiropractor's school - a long way off from his eventual calling as a professional poker player. Meanwhile, Jill worked in the mortgage business, refinancing people's homes for them. It made her enough money to be independent and happy. Bill and Jill met in the months following his divorce, and hit it off as friends quite well. They started as friends, and stayed this way for about two years. But their relationship started to grow and build quite quickly. They eventually got married in 2005, but their relationship was one of devotion and obsession long before that. It was built on lies, secrets, fraud, and a desire to become better and more fabulous than the lives that they were currently leading.

Their relationship worked because, by Jill's own words, they discovered that they were able to get whatever they wanted out of people. However, their reasons were far different. Jill was able to manipulate the people around her because of what she described as "a need to survive." On the other hand, Bill did what he did out of, what Jill described as, "a need to conquer." In stark contrast to Jill's desires, Bill wanted to to be the most superior and successful person to walk into a room.

Their driving desires were far different, but they worked together all the same. Two master manipulators joined together to form a power couple that would lead them both to their eventual ends. Despite his good life, Bill wanted more. He longed to be one of the richest, most powerful people in the room when he walked in, and Jill was able to help him get it. Jill's inheritance money and her job as a refinancing for mortgages allowed her to live the lavish lifestyle that her partner craved. Even in the beginning of their relationship, the two worked together to manipulate whatever system was set up against them.

The Bill and Jill began their partnership in crime not long after they got together. Bill was going through a custody evaluation with his ex-wife. Both Bill and his ex-wife had been in a custody battle over their nine year old daughter for some time, perhaps all the time that Bill and Jill had known one another. Bill's child support payments would have been $4,000 given to his wife - but Bill asked Jill to re-worked his income in the books so that it looked as if he was being paid less than he actually was. Jill had software that was used to prepare your own tax returns. She showed him that she could alter the returns, and that brought bill out of the rage that had consumed him over the possibility of giving his ex-wife four grand in child support. Jill's solution was a savior - together, Bill and Jill worked their magic to cut down Bill's earnings.

Or was it magic? Jill's life story with Bill was left behind in a ten-page suicide note. While Jill Rockcastle never managed to go through with the planned attempt, the note leaves behind sordid and intimate details of their lives. The beginning of their schemes apparently started with a threat. In her note, Jill describes the first arrangement together, shedding more light on the custody scheme. At first, Jill refused Bill's request to arrange his income so that it looked as if he were earning less than he actually was. But then, Bill began to threaten her. A few days before the court hearing, Jill held the phone against her ear, listening to Bill bellow at her from the other end - screaming about how badly he needed her to do this for him. Like many women in her position, the threats and shouting worked, and Jill conceded to the plan.

And that plan also worked. The morning of the court hearing, Jill gave in and fixed the tax return documents to reflect a much lower income that Bill was truly earning. Their first scheme allowed for Bill to pay only $1,800 in child support - less than half of the proposed amount. In her 10 page letter, Jill wrote, "We began living without rules and not afraid of consequence." After all, what an exhilarating moment - to break the law and get away with it. It's no wonder that Jill and Bill became addicted to the thrill of it all. Not to mention, the money that came rolling in with it.

Bill Gustafik eventually opened up his own office in Antioch. Jill worked there with him, though her job behind the scenes was a bit different. She fixed the books in order to subtly increase the profit made between them. Jill was also instructed by Bill to finance real estate deals for some of the patients that came into Bill's chiropractor's office, in order for the income to go directly to Jill. The money that they made together was more than enough - and at the same time, it was nowhere near enough.

While Bill had his own talents when it came to these schemes, it was Jill who was the mastermind. In 2004, Bill took over one of this offices in Hayward, becoming the owner. Jill was the one who helped him purchase the entire building, and Jill was the one who helped him buy the building as an LLC, so that the purchase would have no effect on his personal credit. Meanwhile, Bill used his own talents in scamming his patients. Person after person, Bill would overcharge and over treat his patients in order to get as much money as possible. While Bill was doing this, it was Jill who was working behind the scenes for him - fixing his books, making sure that Bill was getting even more money than he worked for.

Jill had her own schemes, too. Independent of Bill, Jill Rockcastle worked deals, financing larger homes with large mortgages. On each home, Jill would get 2% or more on each one - that meant on a deal that was $700,000, Jill would take home $14,000. This allowed Jill to work less than Bill. In fact, she only worked once or twice a month. Even $8,000 was more than Jill usually spent in a month. While she was content with their level of riches, Bill wasn't. He wanted more, and with Jill at his side, he was determined to get it.

Bill wanted more of of life - even more than his 7 am to 7 pm lifestyle of scamming patients and fixed books was giving him. Bill began to obsess over getting on television. He wanted to play poker, and he wanted to do so on TV. Despite his already lavish lifestyle, Bill wanted more than just that. He wanted global recognition. Jill went along with it - after all, she had the time, and she has the devotion to Bill.

The note that had been left behind, written in Jill's own words, describes how it was around this time that the two of them went off to Las Vegas together - a city full of glittery lights, casinos, gambling, and eventual devastation. It was in October of 2004 that Jill followed

Bill to Las Vegas. As she puts it, their move to Las Vegas was "the beginning of the con." Bill began to live the lifestyle that he believed he deserved - one that was lavish, with extravagant spending. It was Jill who continued to make it all possible, and Jill who continued to watch on. She helped him buy two houses, and get his extravagant car. Everything that Bill had and wanted was because of Jill. Without Jill Rockcastle, he would still be stuck, paying the $4,000 of child support to his ex wife. Bill's desire to be rich in a visible way left Jill vying to make herself worthy of him - she got plastic surgery, enhancing herself to look just like another one of Bill Gustafik glittering trophies.

Jill Rockcastle's letter reveals an even darker side of Bill - one that she, alone, was privy to. There was a time, undisclosed by the note, simply "two years ago", when Jill and Bill had Bill's daughter with them during Christmas time. Jill exposes the man Bill had been. All the time that they had been together, Jill had helped fix everything so that Bill would not have to pay the proposed amount to his ex-wife for child support. Despite Jill's abilities, Bill still wanted to problem gone once and for all. Jill described, in a note to Bill's ex wife, in a chilling lack of detail, that Bill had attempted to have his ex-wife and his ex mother in law killed.

An attempted assassination that didn't go through - the man had taken the money and bolted, leaving Bill both without his money, and Jill with the lasting impression of the lengths that Bill would go to. In Jill's note, she described she believed the Bill felt no love. In her note, Jill says, "He knew deep down that he could not care for someone. [...] he didn't feel love. [...] he didn't feel compassion." This was the man that Jill had been living with for so long. If this man would attempt to put a hit out on his ex wife, there's no telling what he would do to Jill if she didn't continue to fund the lifestyle to which Bill was becoming accustomed.

Jill Rockcastle and Bill Gustafik were living a life that Jill's note described as "the life of fake millionaires". In Las Vegas, Bill finally began to play poker just as he had been obsessing over. The problem arose that Bill wasn't very good. In fact, his first night playing saw that Bill lost nearly ten thousand dollars. Their life together in Las Vegas wasn't everything that it seemed. The money was running out. Together, they were going broke. Their schemes continued on, the con growing and growing, until neither of them had complete control over what they were doing. The new schemes began with getting people to give Jill money. After all, Bill was still struggling with his ex-wife's custody battle. If he obtained more money, it would be scrutinized for child support. So it was Jill who ran the scams, and Jill who brought in the money.

The newest scam to get money was selling fake real estate. Jill allowed the cognitive dissonance get the better of her. Even some of the people who were supposedly their friends fell victim to Bill and Jill - there was nothing and no one that they couldn't con when they put their heads together. All the while, Jill told herself that she was helping out. Even if what they were doing was wrong, Jill was devoted to Bill. She loved him, and she wanted to help him. How could she say no? After all, they had left their lives behind, left behind Bill's doctor's offices, all for the bright light and excitements of Las Vegas. Bill wanted to be a high roller, and for a short while, Jill was rich. She allowed herself to block out the things that they were doing. In her letter, she says, "That's how I lived with my sick self."

But Bill was spending money faster than Jill could bring it it. He began to do drugs, and Jill would watch, dispassionate, as Bill would do lines of cocaine and play online poker. They were running out of money faster than Jill could replenish it. He would play a poker tournament and lose upwards of $15,000. Jill was a gambler as well, but she was better at it than Bill. She wasn't a poker player - rather her game of choice was Roulette. Jill could easily win thousands upon thousands of dollars. But, as quickly as Jill won $20,000 at Roulette, Bill would take it again. She would barely have time to text him of her winnings before he would come from the poker room, take it, and lose it again.

Jill began to squirrel money away. She knew that there was no possible way that they could keep going on like this. She kept money hidden from Bill, giving it to her children - both grown, at the time - if they ever needed it. Bill was beginning to get frustrated and desperate. Jill tucked away her money, and pulled several more scams that kept Bill in earnings to spend and lose. It was Jill who went to the bank to deposit money in order to keep their bills paid while Bill continued hemorrhage winnings. It was always Jill who had to deposit the money. Every once in awhile, Bill would give her cash and have her deposit it in the bank. The money had to look as if it were coming from Jill, least Bill's ex-wife become aware that Bill was skimming on his custody payments.

Jill was starting to breakdown. Her life had been reduced to running scams, telling lies, and bowing to Bill's whims. Jill knew that she had to stop Bill somehow. In her ten page suicide note, Jill describes, "I"m going to skip so many things in an effort to shorten this but my life was a constant hell for the last year. I'm going to skip all the lawsuits [...] All the tax notices. All the bounced checks. All the drugs." It was this hell that drove Jill to feeling as if she was the only one who was able to put a stop to Bill. She made phone calls to friends and other connections, feeling an ever overwhelming desperation. Jill even made a call to her attorney, desperate for someone to help her and get her out of the situation - her attorney only told her that Bill was addicted to gambling, and that the only thing to do is to wait until he has nothing left. But waiting was not something that Jill could, or would, do.

Jill took it into her own hands to stop bill, after having gone to the doctor and found out that the stress of the situation has started to give her shingles. At 7:30 in the evening, police received a call from an anonymous person, telling them of a dead body. When police investigators arrived, they wound Bill Gustafik dead. His body was in the master bedroom, and a kitchen knife was stashed away in the trash bin. The police had very little contention among them about who the suspect could be. Upon first glancing at the scene of the crime, they immediately suspected Jill Rockcastle.

The crime was quick. For Jill Rockcastle, killing her husband was not a drawn out plan, with weeks in the making. Nor was Bill Gustafik's death one that caused the police to go on a chase for their suspect. The night before what Jill called "the incident", the couple got into an argument - like most of the arguments in these days, it was about money. The day previous, Bill was leaving for the Bellagio Hotel, located in Las Vegas. He wanted Jill to pay his buy-ins for a poker tournament, and he wanted her to bring $30,000 for him to use. But Jill didn't bring the money. Either she couldn't get it, or she refused to. When she got to their shared Las Vegas condo, the couple began to argue. But the fight didn't end there. After going to sleep angry, Bill and Jill awoke in the morning to continue the same argument. Bill continued to demand Jill to give him money that he could play with. This time, Bill demanded $7,500 from her. Still, she refused.

Bill's aggression began to build. Jill's fears were starting to become realized. He was threatening to kill her, along with her ex wife. It was then that Jill made an attempt to leave. As she went to leave, Bill physically blocked her with his body. He forced her back from the door and into the kitchen. Jill grabbed a knife from the kitchen to defend herself, fearing for her life. The note described how Jill was afraid that Bill would kill her, just as he had said that he would do. She couldn't escape him, though. He simply kept coming for her, and Jill did what she knew would stop Bill once and for all. She swing the knife into his chest, holding the weapon with both hands. When he went down, Jill still had the knife in her hands. In her own words, Jill says she "just snapped".

Jill stabbed him over fifteen times. Just like that, Bill was gone. There was no grand plan. After years of scamming, scheming, lying and cheating, Jill was done. The story of Bill and Jill ends the way so many women's stories have ended - a dead husband, a knife in their hands, years of fear and abuse behind them. While the story leading up to Bill's death involved so many lies, and so many cons, the story of his death is an anticlimactic one. A death that Bill wouldn't have been proud of - the only thing that made him notable in death was the same that made him notable in life: his wife, Jill. And though Bill had gone out as many men do, stabbed and left for dead, it was Jill Rockcastle that made sure everyone would remember his name, and her own.

After he was dead, Jill cleaned up after herself, cleaned herself up, and fled from the condo. Just like that, Bill Gustafik was dead and Jill Rockcastle was on the run. She had stopped him, just as she knew that she had to do. It was then that Jill Rockcastle disappeared, and on the Monday after Bill Gustafik's death, Jill Rockcastle sent an email to her friends, family and various business partners. The email included ten pages of a suicide note. The note goes in depth on all of Jill's struggles throughout her time of having known Bill, and all of the things that had happened to her. The note describes Bill's struggles with his gambling addiction, and many of the scams and schemes that they had performed today. It was, essentially, ten pages of confessions, implicating herself in all of the things that she and Bill had done together. But, it was always a note to tell everyone goodbye.

In her email, Jill wrote: "This is my final statement done to help all the people affected by my actions [...] and the results of whatever happen to them in our aftermath. I'm writing this so that each person that receives it will identify with the time period in which your experience occurred with him and I and can have some of the why [...] answered. I am not trying in anyway to justify a single thing in here. I am not looking to clear my name or actions. I have already done the most final things possible to stop us from hurting anyone else."

The email was a suicide note, one that was meant to tell everyone that nothing that she and Bill had done would ever touch them again.

She alludes here to Bill's death, and to what she had planned to do in order to "stop us" from continuing on how she had been.

Of course, police investigators couldn't let Jill Rockcastle get away with what she had done by allowing her to kill herself. An attempt to find Jill where she had fled was made, first by searching her home in San Ramon that she had kept with Bill. The Las Vegas police called the San Ramon police and urged them to go to the home that Jill and Bill had owned together in San Ramon, in order to arrest her or take her to the hospital, depending on how far she had gone through with her plan to end her life.

However, police investigators were shocked to find that Jill Rockcastle was not in her home in San Ramon. When the police broke down her door, there was no one. Another anonymous call was given to the Las Vegas police, this time urging them on to another location, this time in San Luis Obispo. The call advised them that Jill could be found at a bed and breakfast by the name of Petit Soleil Bed and Breakfast. The San Luis Obispo police searched the small establishment, and found her in her room. She was unconscious, having attempted to end her life with an overdose , just as she had stated that she would in her email.

It was three days after the initial murder when Jill Rockcastle was finally found and apprehended. After the email had gone out, people had begun coming forward with stories of their experiences with Jill Rockcastle and Bill Gustafik. Some people were adamant that Bill didn't deserve what he had got, even if he was a scammer and a cheat. Many people also described Jill has being aggressive herself, with a cocaine habit that matched her husband's. More and more people came forward to tell their stories about how the couple had cheated them out of property and money.

It was Jill's email that had described Bill as aggressive and dangerous, detailing all of the ways in which she was afraid of him. As more people came out of the woodwork as victim's of Jill and Bill, a new light was beginning to be shed on Jill herself. Jim Rivera, one of Bill Gustafik's closest friends from when they were younger, described the Bill in Jill's letter as "inconsistent" with the man that he had known his whole life. Another anonymous friend, this one of Rockcastle, described Jill has being the one to lure Bill into a relationship. Jill was the mastermind, people who knew the couple said. In court, attorneys said that Jill Rockcastle showed no signs of battered woman's syndrome, as both her own public defender and ten page email tried to claim.

Perhaps no one will ever know the truth of what happened between Bill Gustafik and Jill Rockcastle. All that is known is the memories of the couple, the memories of Bill, and the email that had been sent to friends, family and business contacts. Jill had intended to be dead after sending that email, so there is no telling what is truth, exaggeration, or fiction, when Jill did not expect to have to answer for her crime, or the story that she left behind.

CALI DOE

Chapter 1

It was a cold, wet morning on November 10, 1979. It had rained nonstop the night before. The dark clouds had cleared seemingly to allow the morning sun to wake up the farmers in Caledonia, a rural area about a half hour's drive from Rochester, New York.

Although he didn't know it at the time, this day would be one that stuck with Wes Clements the rest of his life.

Wes Clements was around ten years old in 1979. He and his father lived and worked on a farm in Caledonia and had risen with the sun that day, happy to see it after a long stretch of rainy weather. The pair was getting ready to go over their cornfields with the ol' combine tractor that morning, but their plans got delayed when they made a startling discovery.

Just inside the borders of their cornfields, the part of their fields that backed up on a nearby freeway, was the body of a teenage girl face down.

"We didn't know at first that it was a dead girl," Clements has said. "We thought it might be some kind of Halloween prank gone wrong, like a balloon that had floated away or something."

In fact, it was the body of Tammy Jo Alexander, but Clements wouldn't know that until over 35 years. At the time, she was just the girl in the cornfield.

The girl in the Clements's cornfield looked like a young teenager. She was petite, about 5 feet 3 inches tall and 120 pounds. She had brown eyes and light brown hair that was bleach blonde at the ends. Her hair was wavy and was just long enough to dust her shoulders.

The girl's skin was tan, she had visible tan lines from a halter top and her face and shoulders were speckled with freckles and acne. She was cute, but not quite old enough to be beautiful yet. She had had plenty more growing still to do before her life was cut recklessly short.

The Clements's also couldn't help but notice the girl's clothing. She was dressed fairly typical for a girl her age—she was wearing a plaid button-up shirt and tan corduroy pants—but her jacket was seemingly unique. It was a man's nylon-lined, red windbreaker jacket with thick, stark black lines running down the arms. Later, a label inside the coat was found marking it as manufactured by *Auto Sports Products Inc.*

Along with typical clothing, the young girl was also wearing jewelry. She had a silver necklace with three small turquoise stones around her neck and two silver keychains attached to her belt loops. The first was shaped like a heart and read *He who holds the key can open my heart.* The other was the key, made to fit a cutout on its heart-shaped companion.

When Wes Clements and his father Harry realized what they were looking at, they immediately called police.

The first responder on the scene was John York of the Caledonia Police Department.

"I was not far away. I arrived on the scene with Harry and his son as we walked to the area where the body was found," said Officer York. "She was laying face down in a cornfield. Somewhat off the road, about 20 yards laying in the corn."

It seems silly to dump a murder victim so close to a popular freeway on paper, but in reality it was almost impossible to see the spot she was left for dead from the road. Corn stalks are tall and grow thickly. The dense vegetation is difficult to see through. Officer York himself needed guidance from Harry Clements and his young son Wes to navigate through the crop to the body.

When Officer York first laid eyes on the girl he thought she may have been the victim of a hit-and-run accident. Maybe a trucker was going a bit too fast and didn't see the girl crossing the road until it was too late. It made sense. However, when he got closer to the body he saw two distinctive gunshot wounds—one on her head and the other on her back. She had been shot than left for dead in the cornfield.

"We secured the area and began an investigation that we thought would be very normal," says Officer York. "But it became anything but a normal homicide investigation."

The young girl had no identification on her, her pockets had been turned inside-out seemingly by her assailant, so she was officially declared a Jane Doe. As her case continued and her identity remained a secret she took to the grave with her, she became known more specifically as Cali Doe after the area she was found in.

Chapter 2

The investigation into Cali Doe's death had the odds stacked against it from the beginning.

First, there was the rain. Caledonia had been soaked by heavy rains that fell consistently for days before the discovery of Cali Doe's body. The whole crime scene and surrounding area was soaking wet, saturated with rain.

Second, there was the location. Caledonia was a small community, but one on the road to bigger places. The freeway that ran through the town and right next to where Cali Doe was found was the 520, a major truck route that connected Canada to the US. Across the road from the farm was also a heavily treed pull-off area where a lot of trucks were known to stop and rest.

Third, there was the fact that she had no identification.

All three of these factors had a major effect on the case. The rain meant that any physical evidence around Cali Doe's body had been either degraded, destroyed, or washed away. The location made it difficult because it indicated that a truck driver may have been involved, meaning that the perpetrator would be from out of town and not known by the locals. The lack of identification meant that investigators had nowhere to start.

In the face of all this hardship though, Officer York stayed positive and focused on what little evidence he did have to work with. He became the lead investigator on the case and stuck with it for decades, even after

Officer York was intrigued by the fact that Cali Doe's skin was so tan. She had had the marks of a halter top or bikini engraved into her skin by the sun. Especially in the face of all the rain Caledonia had gotten lately, the recent tan mean that Cali Doe was probably from a sunnier part of the country—that or she'd just got back from vacation.

Initially, Officer York thought that he would find a missing person's report matching Cali Doe's description when he began looking in the larger area of Livingston County but he never did.

"We thought if we looked in Livingston County we would get an identification the next morning," said Officer York. "If we put it on the television, someone would pick up the phone and someone would say I know that girl."

No such phone call ever came.

Wes Clements and his father Harry, who had discovered Cali Doe's body on their farm, were quickly cleared from the case. They were questioned separately and provided matching accounts of their morning and night before. The father and son also willingly provided shoeprint samples and other forms of forensic samples when requested.

Little physical evidence was found where Cali Doe's body had been left in the cornfield, but more evidence was found in the surrounding area. After the coroner's report revealed that Cali Doe had been shot in the back in the spot she was found, but she had first been shot in the head somewhere else.

Investigators tried to recreate Cali Doe's pathway through the cornfield to the road and found an area along the roadside that appeared to be stained with blood. Cali Doe had been shot in the head unaware on the side of the freeway and then dragged into the field where she was shot in the back once more for good measure.

Investigators tried to search the surrounding cornfield and areas along the freeway to find more evidence such as a discarded ID card or purse contents but retrieved nothing.

The coroner's report revealed a few other clues about the identity and last day of Cali Doe's life such as the girl's last meal. Within an hour of being killed, Cali Doe had eaten a simple meal of corn, potatoes, and boiled ham. Eatery food. It filled you up, but it wasn't fancy.

It hurt Cali Doe to chew her final meal. A molar on her left side seemed to have had a cavity for over a year and one on the right was even worse. To have either fixed would've meant the first trip to the dentist for the sixteen-year-old.

While her last meal seems like inconsequential evidence, it lead to one of the most important discoveries in the early days of the Cali Doe investigation. It lead Officer York and his team to Marge Bradford, a waitress at the Lima Diner 25 minutes down the road from the Clements's cornfield.

Chapter 3

After the coroner assigned to Cali Doe's case revealed that the young girl had eaten a typical diner meal of corn, potatoes, and boiled ham within an hour of being killed, Officer York was struck with an idea.

"We wanted to find something or someone who had seen Cali Doe right before she ended up in the cornfield. I assigned investigators to then drive down the road and visit every rest stop and restaurant they ran into." Said Officer York.

Officer York and his team visited over 70 restaurants. Eventually, they came across the Lima Diner, which was nestled into nearby Lima's downtown—an intersection dubbed by locals as *The Four Corners*.

In 1979 Marge Bradford was a waitress at the Lima Diner. She was 21-years-old and lived in a trailer down the street, close enough for her to walk to work.

On November 11, 1979, Bradford met Officer York and his team when she arrived to work around 2pm. They asked her if she had seen anyone matching Cali Doe's description two nights earlier and astonishingly, she had.

November 9 was a Friday, and every Friday night at the Lima Diner was fish fry night. At about 8:30pm, two people walked into the restaurant and sat in Bradford's section.

"I'd never seen them before. They were strangers," Bradford told the officers. "On Friday nights you usually got the regulars, you know, always the same people for fish fry night. Most of them were my friends."

But these two weren't. The pair had arrived in the restaurant fairly late for a fish fry night, which was a busy time for the small diner. By the time Cali Doe and her mystery companion walked into the restaurant almost all the locals had cleared out since the dinner rush, but it was still too early for the bar crowd to start shuffling in. They were just about the only two people in the restaurant besides staff at the time.

According to Bradford, Cali Doe's companion was a man around 25-years-old, was around six feet tall, and had light brown curly hair and glasses.

"They seemed know each other but didn't seem like they were boyfriend and girlfriend. More like brother and sister or something like that," Bradford said. "That was the impression I got."

Bradford told police that there didn't seem to be anything unusual about the two's time in the diner. The young girl matching Cali Doe's description seemed happy, she didn't seem nervous or upset about anything. She in fact spent most of the time laughing with her companion.

Nothing about the pair struck a chord of worry in Bradford or any of the other staff, which in itself is one of the strangest aspects of the case. Cali Doe was found murdered only eight-and-a-half miles up the freeway.

"Why would you buy someone dinner and kill them 25 minutes later and throw them in a cornfield? I had never made any sense to me. She didn't act worried at all. Or afraid." Said Bradford.

Investigators worked with Bradford to draw up a composite sketch of the man seen with Cali Doe and the sketch was spread all around the county but it never lead to a suspect. They remained confident that Bradford had seen the actual Cali Doe though as Bradford had been able to describe her distinctive jacket in detail. She also described the meal she served to the young girl that night—it had been a simple meal of corn, potatoes, and boiled ham.

Chapter 4

After Marge Bradford, a waitress at the Lima Diner, was able to prove she had seen Cali Doe alive and well and with a companion within an hour of her death, investigators and lead officer John York were confident they were now on the right path to discovery who Cali Doe was as well as how she ended up dead in a cornfield. They were wrong.

Bradford's description of Cali Doe's companion turned up no new leads, and the diner provided them with no new information about Cali Doe except for the direction she had been travelling in. The case began to lose heat quickly, investigators had nowhere to go with the case.

"Typically within a week somebody's called. A friend, a family member, somebody has reported her missing and launch the missing person report. But a week went by, months went by, nothing." Said Officer York.

So Officer York began searching in new places, and remained the primary detective on the case for decades to come despite being promoted to the Livingston County Sheriff's department in 1989. No one worked harder on the case than York, who had felt the weight of the young girl's case since he was first led into the Clements's cornfield.

"The investigation began for me in November 1979 and continued for 36 years," said now Sheriff York. "You like to take pride in your work and think you're going to get resolve and justice for every victim. It's not realistic but you believe that. My personal belief was that Cali Doe had the right to better. She deserved better."

The more the years passed, the more York wanted answers for the young girl. He began to take the case personally, as it soon became the only unsolved case he had ever worked on. He became obsessed.

York spent months alone trying to dig up information on Cali Doe's distinctive jacket. It didn't look like it belonged to her, so he was hoping it could've been her killer's. Plus, it looked different than any jacket you could buy in a typical department store. It looked unique, unique enough to lead directly to one individual person—or so York hoped.

York spent weeks trying to locate the jacket's manufacturer, *Auto Sports Products Inc.*, which was named in the jacket's tag. He sent photos of the jacket along with the company's name to the FBI and received no response. He wrote letters to every State Senator in the country as well. One Senator recognized the label, and replied to York. The manufacturer was a mushroom farmer in California.

Again, York was initially hopeful but couldn't be for too long. The mushroom farmer, as it turned out, had been the Vice President of a major car manufacturer in the late '70s. He had made several thousands of the coats, which were given away to auto sports companies and other car manufacturers as a promotional item. There was no way to tell where the coats had been sent and who had received them. It was another dead end.

York remained ever determined, but he now began to scramble. He had artist renderings of Cali Doe made from autopsy photos and sent them all over the country along with the sketch of her companion from the night she was killed. He took the story international to Mexico, and began personally talking to police departments across the country, begging them to double check their missing persons and runaway reports. Nothing pertinent ever came up.

In the late 1970's hitchhiking was fairly common and sadly so was occurences of hitchhikers becoming vulnerable targets for predators. That's why York decided he had to consider that Cali Doe had been killed by the worst of the worst—a serial killer. He wanted to talk to some serial killers that had modus operandis that matched the evidence in the Cali Doe case. One of those men were Henry Lee Lucas.

Henry Lee Lucas was a serial killer from Waco, Texas who liked to confess to murders he didn't commit—many of which remain attributed to him today. Officer York decided to interview Lucas in 1984. Lucas, in his normal style, confessed to the crime but was unable to provide any new facts about the murder and got several facts about the murder incorrect during his confession to York, including the colour of Cali Doe's distinctive jacket.

After talking to Lucas, York was convinced he had played no role in the murder and crossed the serial killer off his list of suspects. Ottis Toole, another serial killer who was a friend of Henry Lee Lucas's, was also interviewed by York. Although Toole's description of events matched the story Lucas had given York, he was also ruled out as a suspect. York believes that both men got what little information they did know about the case from newspapers and the TV as the case was widely publicized across the nation thanks to York's efforts.

Although York refused to give up on the case, it would be over 20 years before any new information emerged.

Chapter 5

In September of 2005, Cali Doe's body was exhumed in order to have DNA samples collected. The hope was she could eventually be identified through a DNA match with any living relatives. It had been 26 years since the young girl's body was found in the cornfield and countless advances in forensic science and investigation practices had been made. Cali Doe's DNA was automatically ran through CODIS, the Combined DNA Index System used by the FBI, on the off chance one of her family members were in the system but unsurprisingly a match was not found.

Cali Doe's DNA was collected by the University of North Texas Center for Human Identification. Despite Cali Doe being buried for almost three decades, they were able to produce a mitochondrial DNA profile for the girl through DNA profiling.

While her body was consumed, Cali Doe also had several of her teeth removed, which were then sent for mineralogical and forensic isotope analysis. This was done because investigators still had no idea where the young girl was from. Luckily, tap water across the US varies in quality because every area of the US has different mineral compositions and combinations. When you drink the water in your own area, the specific mineral compositions leave markers in your bones and teeth as they develop. Using this modern forensic science, investigators were able to prove for the first time that Cali Doe was definitively from the Southern region of the US.

This evidence was strengthened in 2006 when forensic palynology was conducted on Cali Doe's clothing. This meant that pollen from her clothing was collected, analyzed, and matched with an area in the US that contained all samples. If an area of the US could be found, that would likely be the area that Cali Doe was from.

The pollen found on Cali Doe's clothing was determined in 2006, and again in 2012, to have originated from California, Arizona, or Florida.Amazingly, nine years after the pollen was first analyzed, the palynology findings would be proven correct when Cali Doe was positively identified in 2015.

Chapter 6

Facebook has been one of the most defining elements of the 2000's since it was made available to the world in 2006. In a very strange way, it also helped uncover the true identity of Cali Doe.

In 2015, a woman that had gone to school with Cali Doe began perusing the social media website looking for old classmates. While she was able to find an account for most of her old friends, she failed to find one for one of her favorite friends from high school, Tammy Jo Alexander.

Tammy Jo Alexander and the woman had attended high school together in Brooksville, Florida. After the summer of '79 Alexander never came back to school, and no one ever really knew why beyond rumours. While she couldn't find any trace of Tammy Jo Alexander on the internet, Alexander's classmate was able to track down Alexander's half-sister Pamela Dyson, who now lived in Panama City.

Dyson wasn't able to provide much information about Alexander's current whereabouts. Alexander had worked as a waitress in a truck stop and had a habit of running away. She liked to hitchhike and would often catch rides with the men she met in the truck stop. One summer, she took a ride to California on a whim with her best friend. She loved travelling and told her folks upon her return that she planned to do it again.

Dyson knew her sister had gone missing in 1979, but her home life at the time left her in the dark about any developments in the case. Alexander and Dyson's mother had been a violent alcoholic who was addicted to prescription drugs and often lashed out at the girls. It was a volatile environment and both young girls did everything they could to avoid confrontations. When Alexander disappeared, Dyson quickly learned that it was not to be spoken about.

But Dyson did believe that her mother had filed a missing persons report so Dyson went with Alexander's classmate to the Hernando County sheriff's office to check in on the report. When they arrived, there was no report on file. It is likely that Alexander's mom wasn't taken seriously when filing the report as Alexander had a history of running away.

Up to this point in her life, Dyson had believed that Tammy Jo Alexander had walked away from her volatile home life to start fresh somewhere else. She pictured her in California, living by the beach with a husband and children. It would've been a loving household, as Alexander remained happy and bright-spirited despite living in a volatile hell.

When Dyson found out no one had looked into what had happened to her sister back in the late 70's she became very worried—the idyllic image she had had of her half-sister crumbled to pieces. She decided to file her own missing persons report. Tammy Jo Alexander was officially listed as missing, and her file was posted into the National Missing and Unidentified Persons System, or NamUs. NamUs is used across America to identify Jane and John Does and to make missing persons information available nationwide.

Along with basic information about her sister and their life, Dyson included an old school photo of Alexander from the year before she went missing. Shortly after Alexander's missing persons profile was entered into NamUs, her photo was recognized by an unbelievable source.

Carl Koppelman was a Californian artist who had spent his life creating artistic reconstructions from unidentified corpses. Officer York had gotten Koppelman to create a reconstruction of Cali Doe both in 2010 and 2014. A year since his last reconstruction of the young girl, he was now positive he was staring at her real face and her real name.

Koppelman immediately emailed the Livingston County sheriff's office, which was still overseeing the Cali Doe case 36 years later even though John York had retired in 2013. The resemblance was confirmed after Dyson's DNA was compared to Cali Doe's taken in 2005. The results were clear—the two women shared the same mother.

Cali Doe was finally identified as Tammy Jo Alexander.

John York, the primary detective on Cali Doe's case for 34 years found the identification to be bittersweet. He was relieved to know that Tammy Jo Alexander wouldn't have to rest unnamed any longer, but it was a stark reminder that they still didn't know who her killer was. The identification of Cali Doe as Tammy Jo Alexander did not bring in any new viable leads, although the as of January of 2017 the case remains classified as active.

Cali Doe had been buried in the Dansville Cemetery in Dansville, New York since her autopsy. Her grave had been marked by a donated headstone inscripted with the name Caledonia Jane Doe and an approximated lifespan.

After Tammy Jo Alexander's identification, Dyson decided to keep her sister buried in peace where she had been for so many years. A proper funeral service was finally conducted for the young woman and a nearby funeral home paid to have the headstone replaced with another that told the true story of the young girl's life.

Tammy Jo Alexander's death was both tragic and uplifting. It is always tragic when a young life is taken in a brutal way, especially when they remain nameless for decades after, but it is equally uplifting to see a community embrace a victim who had no one else to stand up for her. The community in Livingston County and Officer John York made sure Cali Doe was never forgotten. And for their efforts, a family and many friends now know what happened to the bright, beautiful, and bubbly Tammy Jo Alexander.

www.ingramcontent.com/pod-product-compliance
Lightning Source LLC
Chambersburg PA
CBHW031439130726

47989CB00003B/1214